SONYASHKA

NORMA COHEN GITTELMAN

ISBN 978-1-63903-913-5 (paperback)
ISBN 978-1-63903-915-9 (hardcover)
ISBN 978-1-63903-914-2 (digital)

Christian Faith Publishing, Inc.
832 Park Avenue
Meadville, PA 16335
www.christianfaithpublishing.com

Printed in the United States of America

I dedicate this book
to the memory of my beloved mother,

Sonia Zitman Cohen

Her determination to keep her family together
had set a standard for generations that followed

Preface

IN DOING RESEARCH FOR THIS book, I reviewed tapes, pictures, maps, spoke with authors, writers from a national Anglo-Jewish magazine, cousins, cousins, and more cousins.

I especially want to thank my cousin Sandy Schiff and Rabbi Myer J. Schwab for helping me find the correct English spelling for the title of this book. I also want to thank my cousin Sheldon Zitman for giving me information about the name changing from Zitefsky to Zitman and my cousin Fran Schusterman for giving me the correct name of her father, Max Gaidal, later changed to Gordon.

Note: My mother's name was Sonia or Sonya. My father's endearing name for her was Sonyashka, hence, the title of this book.

Introduction

1791, CATHERINE THE GREAT OF Russia acquired territories with large Jewish population from the Polish Lithuanian Commonwealth and Ottoman Empire from 1772–1815. These Jews were forbidden to migrate to Russia.

Territories were designed in Ukraine called the Pale of Settlement by the Imperial Russian Government. Within these settlements, Jews were reluctantly permitted to live. More and more Jews migrated. Tensions turned into fights; fights turned into destruction of property, killings, and terror. That was the beginning of the pogroms.

In 1894, Nicholas II became the czar of Russia, and Jews began migrating into Russia. The May Laws of 1882 (the anti-Semitic law) were still in effect and not abolished. Uprising escalated from cities to the small villages and shtetls. These uprisings were called pogroms.

This law allowed officers of the state (constables) and soldiers to invade towns, cities, and shtetls. These soldiers began riots and destroyed properties. They indiscriminately killed the men of the town, raped and killed women and children. In the 1905 pogrom in Yekaterinoslav (today called Dnipro), they killed mostly female children.

Two million Jews fled the Russian empire between 1880 and 1920. Many fled to the United States and United Kingdom.

PART 1

Sonyashka
(Sonia)

THIS IS WHERE MY STORY begins.

In this country called Ukraine, in the shtetl called Hajsyn, lived a Jewish family named Zitefsky Raisa (Rose) Saminsky Zitefsky and her husband, Avraham (Abraham) Zitefsky. Their family consisted of two daughters (Sonia, age twelve; Anna, age ten) and two sons (Solomon, age eight; Louis, age six).

Avraham and Raisa owned the only general store in the town of Hajsyn. Avraham was a warm, friendly man, the kind that said "you do not bother me, and I will not bother you." Many shoppers would come to purchase supplies, food, and sundry items on credit. These customers would pay for the merchandise later. This system of buy now, pay later would ingratiate Avraham to the townspeople of Hajsyn. This included the constable.

On a cold snowy day in January, the constable, with his army of soldiers, invaded Hajsyn. Avraham knew this pogrom was imminent. When he heard the first gunfire, he took his two daughters to the outhouse. He said, "Girls, do not open the door for anyone who knocks unless you hear my voice."

The Pogrom

"Papa, it smells in there," Anna said.

Sonia told her, "Sha, Anna, I am here with you. We will sit here like Papa said until he comes for us. Please do not cry."

This siege went on for two days, and much damage was done to the shtetl, but the general store was not totally destroyed. The night after the invaders left, Avraham and Raisa spent cleaning up. They restored as many groceries that were salable, then restocked the shelves.

Avraham and Raisa walked back to the house. They sat down in the kitchen over a glass of tea. They were discussing what had transpired during the last two days and nights.

Avraham said, "We must send Sonia and Anna away from here. It is dangerous for them to remain in Hajsyn."

Raisa responded, "The only place is America. My sister Pessy writes to me. It is safe in America." Raisa reflected, touched Abraham's sleeve, and started to cry. Abraham held her in his arms until she regained her composure.

He said, "We must not tell the boys. They would want to go. We need to keep this between us. I must confide in Boris Vanko (the constable) to solicit his help. He is a good friend and can be trusted. I will explain to Sonia what we are planning. She must know how we are going to make this happen. She will have responsibility for Anna."

Raisa thought for a minute. "This is a big responsibility for a young girl. Remember she is only twelve."

Abraham laughed. "I have seen Sonia take on many problems in the store. She is a smart girl. She will know what to do."

Raisa smiled. "I will write my sister in Philadelphia. She must know what papers the girls will need to enter America. They will also need papers to go through the border crossing at Lipscani into Moldova. They will have to show these papers in order to board the train for Bucharest."

"We have much to do in a short time, Raisa. This must be done while the river is still frozen solid."

"Papa, what are you and Mama doing up so late? I heard your voices so I came down. Is everything replaced on the shelves?

"Yes," Raisa answered.

"You should have called me. I would have helped you."

"Sonia, we were just talking about a trip you and Anna are going to take. We decided that a trip to America to see Mama's sister would be exciting."

"All by ourselves?"

"Sonia, it is very late. Go to sleep. We will talk about this later. Do not tell anyone, not even Anna. She will be told when the trip is planned."

"Yes, Papa."

"Good night. Sonia, Don't I get a hug and a kiss?"

"Oh, Papa!"

"Raisa, I must go to the trading exchange in Podil. I must arrange for small gold Ukrainian as well as Romanian coins. They will also need gold necklaces. Why don't you write to Pessy the girls will be coming to America."

Avraham reopened the store. The family helped serve the customers. Family life resumed, except Avraham was conspicuously absent at times. Every evening, Raisa and the girls would be sewing pockets in the girls' underwear, winter hats, dress sleeves, and pockets of their winter coats. Raisa made a pouch for each of the girls to wear around their necks. This was for their Eastern Slavic customs pass. This had to be safe. Little by little, Avraham would explain to the girls the trip they were going to take.

The December winds were blowing. Snow had started to fall. The river was beginning to freeze solid. Raisa was praying that the river was frozen solid by the end of December. She was concerned that the weather would get severe, and crossing the river would be dangerous. The winds on the river could toss two small girls around. How would Boris control this?

She was anxiously waiting for the letter from her sister explaining where the girls would live in Bucharest. The letter finally arrived. Pessy explained she has a friend, Esther, that could not complete her trip to America. She now lived in Bucharest. Pessy went on to explain that Esther had a young daughter about the same age as Sonia. Her name happened to also be Sonya. Pessy then asked if Esther's daughter could travel to America with Sonia and Anna. Esther also wanted to know if the girls had the proper traveling papers to enter Bucharest.

Raisa wrote their papers were fine. They would have no problems. Raisa responded to her sister that Esther's daughter could travel with the girls. She would let her know when the girls would approximately be on their way to Bucharest.

Raisa thought to herself, *The hardest journey would be getting across the frozen river.* The second problem was securing papers for two young girls traveling alone. These papers were needed at the border checkpoint between Moldova and Romania. Now that the travel plans were in place, Abraham and Boris had to meet to work out a realistic story to tell the authorities.

Avraham said, "Raisa, Boris comes every Saturday for food and supplies. When the store becomes empty, I will approach him."

That Saturday, Boris came as usual.

Avraham asked, "Would you mind helping me bring some of your large packages from the barn to your cart, Boris?"

As the men left the shop, Boris said, "What is on your mind, Avraham? I have no packages."

"I do have a very large favor to ask. The pogrom that transpired here last month has Raisa extremely upset. She now wants the girls to go to her sister in America."

"I am sorry I had to destroy some of your barn. As constable, I had to do damage to your place as well. You are aware that I would never harm your children."

"I am aware."

"Avraham, I will have to think this out. The river is frozen solid in Moldova near my sister. I will need supplies, a wagon. I may need help to cross the river."

"When do you want this to happen?"

"As soon as possible."

"When can you develop a plan and arrange for help"

"I will let you know in a few weeks. I have to meet with my sister. That is all I will tell you of my plans. When the officials come to question you, I want you and the family to be honest in your answers. Be careful when talking while the boys are around."

"Boris, you know I trust you."

"We would never want you in jeopardy."

"The boys will be upset. They are not aware of this trip. I will tell them after the investigation by the police. They will not know until you tell me the girls are safe."

"My friend, we will have everything in place when you come."

"Sonia's valise will have a package with instructions for your sister. She will also be informed as to where the girls' journey should end. There will be a package just for your sister."

"Avraham, I believe I should be ready by the last week of this month," Boris said. "Expect me back in two weeks." Then he was off.

The Trip to Podil

IT WAS A COLD BLEAK winter morning when Avraham left his house. The short walk to the barn gave him a chill. He thought as he saddled his horse, *This will be the last thing I have to complete for the girls' trip, traveling to the trading exchange in Podil to pick up the coins.* Albert had written Avraham that the package had arrived and was waiting for him.

Avraham was glad he was the guest of Albert's for the night. He thought, *I am glad I packed my heavy sleeping gown with my furry slippers.* Albert's floors were very cold. As he was about to mount his horse, Anna came running out.

"Papa, Papa, you forgot the food we packed."

"Thank you, Anna. I'm glad you saw this sitting on the table before I left. I would be hungry and thirsty. Now hurry up. Go back into the house. It is very cold and damp out here."

"Okay, Papa. Can I give you a kiss?"

"Oh, Shana, anytime."

As Avraham was riding along the road, he began reminiscing about his girls when they were babies, when they started to walk and talk. *I will never forget Sonia's beautiful blue eyes when the midwife put her in my arms for the very first time. She opened those blue eye and looked at me. I knew this one had my heart forever. I am a very lucky fellow—two boys and two girls and a beautiful wife.*

Avraham spotted the rest stop. His stomach told him it was time to eat. He found an empty table, dismounted, and tied his horse. He took out the food box Anna had given him. Inside the box was half of a chicken, two slices of bread, and a bottle of cold tea. There was a note from the girls telling him they had made the sugar cookies. There was a special note from Sonia wrapped around one of his cigars.

The morning turned into afternoon. Avraham was now beginning to see the principal buildings of the Ukraine government. As he got further into the city, he recognized the rectangular paths of the streets and the old merchant trading exchange. He was grateful he finally arrived. He tied his horse to the post, then entered the exchange. Albert saw him immediately. He came running to greet him.

"Welcome, old friend. It is so good to see you. Tell me, how is Raisa and the family? I heard about the pogrom."

"Albert, let's talk about it tonight."

"Yes, we will talk at dinner. Enjoy your drink. I will get the package I put together for you. Then we will go to my house where you can relax. You will be able to enjoy a hot glass of tea."

Albert escorted Avraham to his desk where they completed the transaction. Albert got his hat and coat. They both were off to Albert's new brick house.

"You have done very well for yourself, a new brick house on a fancy street."

"The best news is, Alana is going to have a baby. Please let her tell you."

Avraham laughed. "Yes, I know. I promise."

They arrived at the new house. Alana met them at the front door.

Avraham said, "Alana you are so beautiful. You look radiant."

"Thank you. Just wait till I show you the kitchen and the bathroom."

As Avraham went around the house with both of them, he was extremely complimentary. He thought to himself, *Raisa would love to have a kitchen like that. Maybe when I get back we will talk about it. That could cheer her up.* The dinner and the drinks were perfect.

While Alana cleaned up, Albert and Avraham talked about what had happened in Hajsyn, the damage, the death of the townspeople.

"The soldiers could care less what they destroyed or who they killed. They disheveled our shop, knocked down shelves, and took apart our barn. They were aware if they completely destroyed the store, they would have no supplies themselves. I was more concerned about our children. The boys went into the underground storage area under the store floor. I took the girls to the outhouse."

"Let us change the subject. I get depressed rehashing those horrible two days, Avraham! It lasted two full days."

"Yes, they wanted to show the commandant that they did a good job."

Alana walked back into the sitting room. The discussion stopped.

Avraham asked, "When is the baby due? Have you picked out a name, be it boy or girl? When do you expect the baby?"

"Wow! We have not thought about some of the questions you ask."

"Well, now you have something to think about. If Raisa and I have any more children, we will run out of names."

There was more small talk when Albert saw that their guest was tiring. He remarked, "I have a busy day tomorrow. It's my bedtime. I will show you to our guest room."

"Thank you."

Avraham was very grateful they went to bed early for he was extremely tired. Tomorrow he had a three-hour ride back home. He also had a busy day at the store.

He awoke as the sun was coming up, Alana had a pot of tea and a roll ready for him on their new kitchen table. He heard Albert coming down the steps.

Still dressed in his bathrobe, Albert said, "I do not go into the exchange today till noon. I work late. I will say goodbye to you here. Go with God."

"Thank you, Albert. for your help...have a beautiful, healthy baby. Let me know when the big day arrives."

A Warm Greeting Home

AVRAHAM'S RIDE HOME WAS TIRING. It began raining a few miles from the house. He and the horse were wet. They could not wait to be home. Sonia was waiting in the barn with a dry warm jacket. Anna had his work shoes.

"Thank you, girls. Where is everyone?"

"The boys are helping mother in the store. Sol is trying to be a salesman like you. Lou is packing the bags. Lou made some kopeks for packing the bags. Sol wants him to share it."

"Girls, I will see if I can help your mother in the store. Then I will close the store."

"Hello, Raisa…can I help you?"

"Yes, you can take over while I make dinner."

"I will take charge of the customers in the store. Sol, you and Lou start to clean up so we can close. Oh, by the way, Lou, I want a share of your kopeks."

"Oh, Papa!"

"Let's close the store, then we will talk."

The last shopper left. It took another half hour before they could officially close. They went into the house. A hot dinner was on the table.

Avraham said as he washed his hands, "Something smells wonderful. I am very hungry."

They sat down, said the prayer, then consumed dinner.

Everyone wanted to know about his trip. He told them, "Alana is going to have a baby. Albert bought a new red brick house with a beautiful kitchen. Alana made a nice dinner."

"Now let's talk about the kopeks that Lou earned. Lou, how many kopeks did you earn today?"

"Six, Papa."

"Well, you earned it. You keep it. I suggest the both of you take turns packing bags. Sol, you pack Monday, Wednesday, and Friday. Lou, you pack bags Tuesday, Thursday, and Saturday. I will pack on Sunday."

Sol said, "Papa, we are closed on Sunday."

"Yes, I know." They all laughed.

Ice Skating on the River

It was a beautiful Sunday, cold but clear. Tomorrow was a holiday. The store would be closed. Avraham said after breakfast, "Let's go ice skating. The river is frozen solid. Remember, children, just stay close to the edge. Do not go into the middle of the river. It may not be frozen solid."

Raisa announced, "I will not go today. This time will allow me to clean our bedroom."

Avraham knew what she meant. "If you wish to stay at home, that is fine. You deserve a rest." He winked to her.

The afternoon passed quickly. Avraham said to Sonia, "Look at that tree limb. We can sit here to take off our skates."

As they started their way home, they sang a few songs, one about a clumsy little bear who walked through the forest. Avraham thought, *This maybe the last time I will see my beautiful girls.*

As they approached the house, they smelled cookies. They knew Mama was busy baking cookies. They put their skates outside before they entered the house.

Lou said, "Who are you baking for, Mama? The cookies smell good."

Raisa answered, "All of my wonderful children."

Avraham said, "Your mother's cookies always smell good. They even taste better."

The day went swiftly. After dinner, they all played a table game. Before they realized it, the time passed quickly. The children said their good night and were off to bed.

Raisa and Avraham waited until they knew the children were asleep. Avraham then asked her, "Did you get all the coins inside the pockets?

"Yes, the necklace will go inside their underclothing. I have no idea when Boris will be back, but we must be ready."

"Raisa, I have to tell you I was much impressed with the kitchen at Albert's house. How would you like to have a new kitchen like Alana's?"

"Really! Avraham, really?"

"Yes. When the girls are safe in Bucharest, you will then be able to enjoy shopping and replacing your kitchen."

Raisa sat much closer to Avraham on the sofa. Raisa said, "You still give good kisses." He kissed her again.

He said, "I can do more than kisses. If this leads to another child, I want to name it." They both laughed.

Boris came to the store early that day for supplies for his troops and their trip.

"Avraham, I need to store supplies in the barn. Could you send Sol and Lou to help?

"They are on their way," he replied as the boys walked to the barn.

Boris asked, "Do you know how to hook the horses to the wagon?"

"Oh, yes. Papa taught us," said Sol as Lou just shook his head in agreement.

"Then show me how you do this."

Boris watched as both boys arranged the bridle and straps on the horses.

"You did a wonderful job, boys. You will soon be old enough to take care of my soldiers' horses."

Sol looked at Lou and winked. They knew their father would never let that happen.

The shop was empty when the boys and Boris entered. Avraham told the boys to help their mother gather wood for the stove while he arranged a new order of food he just received.

Boris said, "Sol, please give this note to your mother." He turned to Avraham. "Are the girls down at the river?"

"Yes. I took them and the boys skating yesterday. Sonia knows exactly where to meet you."

Boris tossed in four bales of hay and the box of food prepared by Raisa for the three-day trip. Boris took off before the boys came back from gathering wood. Avraham returned to the store. He finished putting items away. The rest of the day went slowly.

Boris drove for a while, then spotted Sonia and Anna sitting on a large branch that had fallen from the tree during a storm. He stopped the wagon near the girls.

"Well, ladies, are you ready for a long journey?" He helped Anna and Sonia into the wagon. He then placed the scarf and one boot near the fallen log. And they were off.

"Avraham, Boris left this note for you."

"Read it to me, Raisa. I am very tired."

You are to go to the federal law enforcement agency late afternoon. Report the girls missing. Tell them the girls went to the river to skate, but they never came back. They will find the scarf and a shoe by the river. We will be well away from that area by then. Do not worry, Avraham. Your girls will be safe.

Reporting the Accident

RAISA CAME IN THE SHOP. She asked Avraham, "Have you seen the girls today.?

"No. They liked ice staking so much. I allowed them to go back today. Raisa, I thought they were home with you, no?"

"I will ask the boys."

"They were here with me in the shop all day. I will close the shop. We have to go to the federal law enforcement agency."

Avraham asked the patrons in the shop to please leave, explaining that the girls were missing.

A few of the shoppers asked, "Where was the last place they went to?"

"They went to the river to ice skate. We were their yesterday. The ice was extremely thick."

Three of the patrons said, "Avraham, you go the authorities. We will go to the river to look for them. We will wait for you and the authorities."

"Thank you."

Avraham took the wagon. The family piled into the front seat. Raisa took out her handkerchief. She held it in her hand. They finally reached the federal building entrance.

Avraham entered first, frantically asking, "Where can I report missing persons?"

"What happened, sir?" asked the officer sitting outside at a desk.

"My daughters went ice skating late this morning, and they are not home. They have never done this before. I have my neighbors looking for them at the river, while I came here to report their absence. We need help now, Is there someone who could help us?

"Yes, I will get the commandant."

"Mr. Zitefsky, what has happened?"

Avraham explained exactly what was rehearsed.

"Did your boys go with them?"

"No, they were working at the store."

"I will get some soldiers to help look for the girls. Take them to the place you were skating yesterday."

When the police and the family arrived at the tree branch, there lay the scarf and the boot. A crowd of neighbors were gathered to help. Some came with lanterns and large candles. We looked till it was so dark. Raisa started to cry which upset the boys.

The officer announced, "I know the Zitefsky family. It is too dark to look anymore tonight. Mr. Zitefsky, take your family home. Please come back to the station house. We would like to speak with you."

Avraham took everyone home, then went back to the law enforcement office. The commandant took Avraham into his office.

"I have bad news for you. One of the soldiers went further into the river and found a large hole in the ice. He found the other boot in the water. I am sorry, but your girls must have fallen into the river. Can I be of any assistance?" asked the commandant.

Avraham thanked him and left the law enforcement office. He was a bit shaken.

Boris really did an excellent job in a cover up. If I did not trust him, I would be concerned. I will not tell Raisa what the commandant told me.

The shop was closed for seven days to sit shiva. The boys were still not aware the girls were alive. They would not be told until the girls reach Bucharest.

PART 2

The Flight in a Hay Wagon

DUSK WAS APPROACHING. THE GIRLS were getting tried. Boris overheard them talking.

"Ladies, we will stop at the next crossing. A friend of mine owns an inn. We will stop there. The food is good. We will sleep there for the night. I told my friend I am taking my nieces back home. We will not be able to have this comfort for the rest of the way. We will save the baskets of food for the rest of the trip."

The girls were excited. They never slept away from home.

Sonia asked, "What shall we say if we are asked about our mother?

Boris thought for a moment. He said, "Sonia, you just smile. You can say, 'We are homesick. We cannot wait to see our mother.'"

They were now a few kilometers to the inn. "Girls, I will pay for your lodgings tonight. Your father gave me money. Do not touch your gold coins until you get to my sister's. Do not get undressed. We will be leaving early in the morning."

They were now approaching the inn. They saw a row of torches lighting the way to the inn. Anna and Sonia got excited. They had never been to an inn. Boris pulled the wagon up to the door. He carried them from the wagon and told them to go to the door and wait for him. He had to put the horses in the barn. As the girls waited, they looked inside the door. Anna and Sonia could not believe their eyes.

"Look at that big room, full of tables, chairs, with many people eating—all at the same time. There are people serving them."

"I see, Anna. We have never seen anything like this before."

"Sonia, are we going to eat here?"

Boris overheard their conservation. Laughingly, he said, "Yes, I am going to have dinner with two beautiful young ladies." He held their valises as they entered the inn.

"Boris, my comrade, my friend, welcome. Who are these lovely young ladies?"

"These are my nieces. My sister was sick. I was taking care of them until she recovered."

"I have a table for you in that out cove. Ladies," the owner said as he pulled out the girls' chairs. Anna and Sonia giggled as they sat down.

"Girls," Boris asked, "what would you like to eat?"

Anna spoke up, "Hot soup with black bread and chocolate cake."

Sonia said, "Anna, that will not be enough to eat. Boris, I will have soup with black bread. Anna and I will share a meat and boiled potatoes dish, but we both will have chocolate cake."

"Ladies, that is a good selection. It will keep you for a while. We will not have time for breakfast. We must be on the road to have the daylight."

They all ate with gusto.

"We have to go to the bathroom. Boris, where do we go?"

"There will be a pot in your room for each of you. When you finish, you put the lid on the pot. The cleaning ladies will take care of it."

"Really, really!" Boris laughed again.

It was difficult to sleep that night. Sonia wondered what tomorrow would bring. The sun came into the room and woke Anna. She started to shake Sonia.

"Anna, stop that. I am awake."

They both sat on the bed, putting their arms around their knees.

Anna asked, "Are you frightened, no?

"Boris makes me feel safe. I never thought he would be so kind."

"I agree," said Anna.

There was a knock on the door.

"Ladies, we must leave shortly. I am going downstairs. I will wait for you outside near the wagon. Please hurry."

When the girls came down, Boris was at the wagon waiting for them as promised. He put them and their valises in the wagon, and they were off again.

"Girls, we will be sleeping in the wagon tonight. I figured we will be at the river the day after tomorrow and crossing the frozen river late in the day. We will meet my sister, and she will tell you the rest of the plan. She will get you transportation to Bucharest. Let us take one day at a time till we cross the river."

Anna asked, "Is the ice thin? Could we fall through the ice in some places? Papa always said be careful of the thin ice. How are we going to know where to step?"

Boris answered her questions calmly. He saw she was getting excited. He did not want to upset her. "Anna, I could ride these horses and wagon across this river. The ice is as thick as the size of our horses. Do not worry!"

"See," Sonia said. She had the same thoughts but decided not say anything.

They drove for a long distance and stopped to feed and rest the horses. The girls opened one of the baskets their mother packed. It was full of goodies—hard-cooked eggs, chicken, black bread, and noodles with cottage cheese. The three of them ate.

Anna said, "I am full."

They opened the dessert box and found the famous cookies that Raisa made.

They climbed back into the wagon with Boris's help and continued on their way. Boris knew the terrain of the area. He had driven to his sister's home, riding his horse across the thick icy river. He knew of a spot to stop for the night. The horses and the girls would be sheltered from the cold night winds. He was concerned. The girls were small and young. He wanted to deliver them to his sister in good health. They drove on till the sunset. Boris found his special spot to stop. He had not heard anything from the girls for a while. He called their names, but no answer. He surmised they were sleeping. He was correct. Each had made a small bed for herself in the hay.

Meeting the Baron

BORIS DECIDED WHILE THE GIRLS were fast asleep he would continue on. He drove till the skies turned black, and the wind started to blow the fallen snow around. He thought to himself, *I better start to look for a spot to stop for the night. The weather may turn, and we will be in trouble.*

As he drove on, he heard a dog barking. The horses were not too happy about this; they started whining. He stopped the wagon. He spotted a large dog standing beside the horses. The dog ran away, then came back barking again. Boris decided to follow the dog to see where he was going. Further down the road, the dog led him to a barn and a small house. The dog barked again while in front of this house. A couple came out to see why their dog was barking. They were quite surprise to find two horses with a wagon at their front door.

Boris said, "I am sorry to intrude, but your dog was barking at us. I thought someone might be in trouble, so I followed him. He led me here."

"Yes, the baron thinks he owns this road. He barks at every one who passes by. Can we help you?"

"I notice you have a barn. Is it possible for us to use your barn for the night? I will be glad to pay you for the night's lodging. My sister was ill. Her two daughters are with me until she recovered. I am taking them home."

"Where are the girls now?"

"They made beds for themselves in the hay and fell fast asleep. I do have to wake them."

Boris called, "Sonia, Anna, wake up."

Sonia jumped up. "I really fell asleep. The rolling of the cart put me to sleep. Anna, wake up. I am up now."

To Sonia's surprise, she found herself in front of a house with a barn, a large dog, and two strangers. Meekly, Sonia said hello. Boris started to explain to the girls.

"I was driving down this road, and out of nowhere, a large dog started barking at the horses. I stopped, then the dog ran away. He came back in a few minutes, barking again. So I decided to follow him. He led me to this house and this friendly couple. I have asked if I could pay to use their barn for the night."

"Oh, oh, forgive me. My wife and I would not mind if you had use of our barn for the night. We would not take your money."

Boris thanked them. "We do appreciate it."

Boris took the girls down from the wagon, parked the wagon, and unhooked the horses. The couple said their names were Max and Sylvia Brusky. They invited them in. Boris introduced Sonia and Anna. Sonia asked if they had eaten.

"We have a basket full of food and would like to share it with you."

Sylvia hesitated, then said, "That would be nice."

Boris went back to the barn, took out both baskets, and returned to the house. Raisa had packed a whole brisket already sliced, along with sliced potatoes and her cookies. The other basket had hard-boiled eggs, butterbrots (an open-faced sandwich), noodles, along with butter and cheese.

Sylvia said, "You have packed a feast."

Boris said, "My wife packed well."

They all ate. What was left they repacked for breakfast the next day. The girls asked many questions about the baron. They enjoyed playing with him.

Boris said, "We have to be on our way early. If you will excuse us, it is time for the girls to retire."

The girls used the outhouse, then said thank you and goodbye to their host. They climbed into the wagon. They fell asleep in the same spots they had made earlier that day in the hay. Boris thanked Sylvia. He went to feed the horses, and he too retired.

Crossing the Frozen River from Ukraine to Moldova

SONIA OPENED HER EYES AND saw the sun coming up over the horizon. She was awakened by Boris singing a Russian lullaby.

As she started to move around, he called her name, "Sonia, Sonia, are you awake?"

"Yes. Are we at the river?"

"Very soon."

"You have a nice singing voice. My mother sang that song to us."

"You should wake up Anna. We will be at the river very soon."

"Anna, wake up."

"I am still sleepy."

Sonia said, "You had better get up and be alert for we are very near the river."

Boris said, "We will stop here and have some breakfast, feed the horses, and be on our way. I want to be at the river while it is still daylight."

They then packed up and were on their way again.

Boris announced, "We are at the river's edge."

He stopped the wagon. The horses seemed restless. They did not like the smell of the river. Boris helped the girls down from the wagon. He took both their valises from the wagon as the girls shook the straw from their hats and coats.

"Now, girls, here is our plan. We will have to put both of your clothes in one valise for I will have to carry Anna and one valise across the river. Sonia, you will carry my ice skates. I will need them to get back across the river quickly. The horses will be restless and need to be fed. We will walk to the middle of the river where my sister Rada (Rahda) will meet us. She will take you the rest of the way. You will both wait at Rada's until the papers your father gave you are cleared for you to go cross the border into Romania. Rada will then get you and Anna on a train to Bucharest. Rada will give you the remainder of the instructions when you are secure in her house."

"Boris, my father told me this, but does she look like Anna or me?"

Boris smiled. "She is as beautiful as you. She has your sky-blue eyes."

Sonia smiled at him and gave him a kiss on the cheek. They started across the cold slippery ice. Sonia fell a few times until she became accustomed to the ice. As they marched across the ice, Boris started singing a familiar song. Anna and I chimed in.

"Anna," Boris said, "you have a beautiful voice."

"Thank you. Our mother did sing 'Pus Va Dah' to us many times."

"Anna, please do not cry now! We must hurry. Boris must get back to feed the horses."

The sun started to come up as they walked. They began to feel warmer.

After a while, they saw a woman waving a red scarf. As they walked closer, Sonia saw how beautiful she was. She did have blue eyes. When they reached her, Boris took Anna off his shoulders. Boris introduced the girls to Rada, his sister. He gave his sister their valise. He hugged her, then said goodbye. He started back across the river on his ice skates. The three of them continued to crossed the remainder of the frozen river.

As they walked, Rada asked, "Sonia, how old are you and Anna?"

"I am twelve, and Anna is just ten."

"We will talk later. I must say you are two very brave girls. Your father must be a kind and wonderful person for Boris does not like many people. He trusts even less."

"He does a lot for the people of Hajsyn and Boris's soldiers when they need boots and coats."

"After we are off this icy river, there is a cove where I hid a basket of food. We will stop to eat before we continue to my house. I want to arrive after dark. We do not need nosey neighbors asking questions."

They finally arrived at the end of the ice-covered river. Rada pointed to the cave where she hid the food basket. Anna and Sonia were so hungry; they ate every last morsel of food in the basket. They rested awhile until it became dusk, then they continued their journey.

Rada said, "Girls, we can continue on our way. It is getting dark. My children will be home soon. Let's clean up and go."

Anna asked, "How far do we have to walk?"

"Not too far."

"Sonia, it is difficult walking in these heavy boots."

"I know, Anna, just a little longer."

"Girls, we must walk a little faster. We are lucky that it is not too dark. We have no candlelight to show us the way."

Sonia asked, "What did Boris tell you about the journey we are going to take?

"He told me you two young ladies are going to America to live with your aunt. Do you know exactly where you are going to be in America? I understand it is a very large country."

"Yes, we are going to be in Philadelphia. My mother's sister, Pessy Cohen, lives in Philadelphia. She has lived there for twenty years. Anna and I are very excited about going to America."

"We are almost there, girls. You must be exhausted. These boots are awfully heavy."

"Boris insisted we wear rubber-soled boots so we will not slip on the ice." Then Anna said laughingly, "Sonia did a good job of falling."

"I don't think that is very funny, Anna."

"Well, you did look funny slipping and ending up sitting on the ice with your feet spread out in front of you."

"Anna, you sat on Boris's shoulders the entire time."

Rada said in surprise, "Boris carried you?"

"She is small. He was concerned she would fall. He needed to get back to the horses immediately."

My brother does have a heart after all, she said to herself.

Meeting Rada's Family

"YOU CAN SEE MY HOUSE from here. It is the red brick house."

Anna was surprised to see a red house.

Rada remarked, "In the city, almost all the homes are of red brick."

As we approached the house, we noticed a bicycle and a small pull cart.

Anna asked, "How many children do you have?"

"A girl your age and a boy, four years old."

Anna went on to ask, "Do you have a husband?"

"Yes, but he is not at home. He is away on business. He is a banker. Ladies, please do come in. Arina, where are you? Aart, Aart, where are you?"

They both answered together, "We are here in the kitchen."

"I have two young ladies I'd like you to meet. Could you please come to the sitting room? Arina and Aart, this is Sonia. This is Anna. They are sisters. They will be our guests for a while. They are on their way to America to live with their aunt. They will be staying in Babushka's (grandmother) room till she returns from her trip. Arina, will you show them to Babushka's room, also where to place their clothes."

The girls thanked Rada, then went off with Arina, while Aart trailed behind.

Aart said to Anna, "Would you like to ride in my wagon? I will push you."

"Thank you, Aart. Maybe later. We have to unpack first."

Arina asked, "Where are you from? We live in Hajsyn, a town in Ukraine."

"Where are you going in America?"

Sonia answered, "A town called Philadelphia."

"How will you get there."

"We were told we must go on a large boat to get to America."

"That sounds like fun. I would like to go with you."

"Maybe when you are older you will come to see us in America."

They unpacked and went downstairs. They had a cold dinner, and Arina and Aart went to bed.

Rada, Anna, and Sonia sat around the kitchen table with a railway time chart that went to Bucharest. There were different local times for each location. It was late, and they were all tired.

"We can discuss some of these details tomorrow. We have to remove all the coins from your clothing. They have to be taken to the bank. My husband will be home tomorrow. He will exchange your coins for Moldova money. It is late. We will talk again tomorrow. Good night."

"Sonia, can we talk?"

"Ann, be quiet. Wait till we get into our room."

"Rada seems like a nice person, but Mama said be careful with the coins. Trust no one."

"If Boris or his sister wanted the coins, they would have taken them before now. Papa said, 'Boris is a good friend. You can trust him.' So I guess we can trust his sister as well.

"Papa told me that he had put money in an account for us at the exchange in Podil where his friend Albert is a part owner. Remember when Papa went away for two days? He went to the exchange in Podil. Anna tell no one what I just told you. The coins are for train fare and whatever we needed to get to Bucharest. Papa gave me a password that I must use when we go to get money from the Bucharest Bank. Papa also gave me a note telling me what bank to visit in Bucharest. Albert will send money when we need it. There is enough for Marseille, along with the boat fare to America. Now go to sleep. I am very tired. Good night. Love you."

"Love you too. Good night."

The sun was coming through the curtains when Sonia heard Anna say, "Go away, Aart. You poked your finger in my eye."

"I am sorry. I wanted to see if you were awake."

"I am awake now."

"Can we go play with my wagon now?"

Sonia saw Anna needed help. Sonia asked, "Aart, where is your wagon?"

Aart replied, "Outside."

"Well, as you can see, Anna is not dressed to go outside. After she gets dressed, she will play with you. Please go downstairs so we can get dressed."

"I am going, Sonia. See you later, Anna."

"It looks like you have a friend, Anna."

Trip to Lipscani Street

"SONIA, THIS HOUSE IS PRETTY. When I get to America, I will want a house like this."

"All right, Anna, one red brick house to order. Now let's go down to get something to eat."

As the girls entered the kitchen, they saw a well-dressed man sitting, drinking a glass of tea with a biscuit. He was talking to Rada about the girls' trip to Bucharest. When they saw the girls, they stopped talking.

"Good morning, girls. This is my husband Leon. I would like to introduce Sonia and Anna. They are on their way to Bucharest. Their father and Boris are good friends. Boris asked me to obtain train tickets, then see them on the train to Bucharest."

"Are they traveling alone, Rada?"

"Yes, they are."

"We have to talk about this. When do you expect this to take place?"

Rada was getting upset. She said, "In about a month or two. No later. They are expected in Bucharest before the end of the following month."

"We have time to discuss this later. It is Sunday. Let's show the girls around town. Arina and Aart will enjoy it as well."

Lipscani is a shopping area where there are all kinds of shops—shoe shops, hat shops, clothing shops. There are places to eat inside the shop as well as outside. There are shops that have toys, pop-up clowns.

Aart said, "Let's go there first please."

Everyone laughed.

"How long have the two of you been standing behind me?"

Arina said, "Not for long."

"Mother, could we go today?"

Leon said, "Yes, Aart, if you promise to behave."

"Oh, yes," Aart said.

"Everyone, get your coats. We will be on our way."

The day was exciting for the girls. They had never seen an area packed with shops. The street was filled with people strolling leisurely. They went into a hat shop. They were looking at the lovely hats.

The shopkeeper said, "You can try on these hats to see if the fit."

"I like this one," said Sonia.

They tried on many hats while laughing at themselves in the looking glass. Sonia tried on a hat with a big rim, a hat that had a bird sitting on the top of it. Anna tried on a hat that had a feather. One hat was too big it fell down over Anna's face. They thanked the saleslady. They walked out of that shop laughing.

Sonia said, "Anna, I had a wonderful time." Anna agreed.

We walked a long time. Neither of us were tired.

Rada said, "Let's stop to eat before we go home."

Aart said, "I did not see the toy shop. I want to go there."

Leon pointed to a shop just across the hat shop.

Aart tugged on Rada's hand. "Let's go there."

"I promised you. So let's all go."

The moment they walked into this shop, they were in awe of all the exciting toys. Everyone went in different directions. Aart pulled Anna with him to see the push-and-pull toys. Anna spotted the doll collection. She left Aart playing with a small train set. She went to the doll collection. She picked up a doll that said "Mama."

She called Sonia, "Come here. Listen to this doll say 'Mama.'"

Rada said, "It is time to go. I will collect everyone and meet you outside."

Leon found an outdoor place to eat. They all jammed through the door. The waiter acknowledged Leon and seated us immediately. The girls were introduced as guests. Anna and Sonia shared a plate of noodles, hard-boiled eggs with cheese. The nice waiter brought a special desert for the family. It was getting dark as they approached the house. Both girls were tired walking.

The girls said, "Thank you for a lovely day."

They excused themselves and went off to bed. They talked about the wonderful day they had.

Anna said, "I will always remember this day."

Discussing Border Checkpoint and Train Tickets

RADA SAID TO LEON, "THE girls are lovely. They are well-behaved."

"Tell me, Rada. Who would send two small girls on a journey by themselves? Boris had them, and now I have the responsibility of them getting to Bucharest."

"They are being sent to live with their aunt. There was a pogrom in the next village. All the young girls were killed. There was a pogrom two months ago in their village. Their father hid the girls in the outhouse for two days without food, just water, to keep them safe. Their father and mother knew the girls had to leave. It is safer for them to leave than stay."

"Well," Leon said, "then let's get them to Bucharest."

"Their mother hid Ukrainian gold coins in their clothes. It was for their tickets to Bucharest. We removed all the coins. Would you take the coins and convert them to currency at your bank? I need that money to buy their tickets."

"How are you going to get them on the train? They are under-age. I want to be with you when you tell them your plans. Is that all right with you?"

"Oh, Leon, you are a softy too." They hugged and proceeded up the stairs to bed.

The next few weeks, the girls played with Arina and Aart. Arina wanted to know what life was like in Ukraine. Sonia explained it was not like the city.

"We have a barn, horses, chicken, and one milk cow named Blacky. She is black and white, spotted. We have two brothers named

Sol and Lou. They do not pay attention to us. They work in our father's general store."

"What does your father sell?"

"We have the only grocery store in the town. We sell food and supplies."

Anna said, "We miss our mother and father. We will all be together when they get to America. Our father promised."

"I know, Anna. We will see them again. We have a job to do. We have to get to America safely so we can help them follow us," said Sonia.

Rada made a delicious dinner. The girls cleaned the dishes, then they played a game at the kitchen table with the family. Rada then said it was bedtime for Arina and Aart.

Leon explained, "When Rada comes down, we will talk about your trip to Bucharest."

Sonia asked, "Do you have our tickets?"

"Yes, Rada has them."

Rada came down after saying goodnight to the children.

"Girls, let's sit around the kitchen table. It is easier to explain your trip. I have your tickets to Bucharest. This is how we are going to get you on the train. You must have an adult with you. I will travel with you till the first stop. You are not from Moldova, so your papers must be checked and signed before you board the train to Bucharest. I will have your papers for the station master to sign. I will give them back to you, put them in the pouch your mother made.

"We will board this train for a few kilometers, and we get off at the stop in Ungheni Prut. There is a five-hour wait for the train to Ungheni Prut Hm. Bucharest station. You will not change trains again. I will get you settled in your seats, then I will get off the train. Your tickets are already stamped, so you do not have to show them again. Remember you must stay on the train till the train master call last stop Ungheni Prut Hm. Bucharest. That is the station in Bucharest. You will be on this train for eight hours, all night long. I will pack food, drinks, and blankets. Sonia, do you understand?"

"Yes, this train will get into the Bucharest station in the morning."

"I gave you my address. When you get to your aunt's friend's house, send me a note. I will write to Boris. He will tell your parents that you arrived in Bucharest."

"When do we leave?"

"Thursday, and you will be in Bucharest Friday. Each of you will have half of the money left. Put it in your pouch with your papers. How long will you stay in Bucharest?"

"We do not know."

"Do you have an address where you are staying?"

"Yes, but Papa told me not to give it to anyone."

"Oh, yes I understand. Then write to me. I will write to Boris. He will tell your parents you are safe. Girls, we will walk to the train station so you can see a train."

Anna said, "I have never seen a train before. We have to go on one."

"You will see one tomorrow."

"Rada, how will you get home?"

"I will take the next train to Lipscani. Now it is bedtime. See you in the morning. Good night."

"Sonia, I am so glad we are going to bed early. I have so many questions to ask," Anna said.

Sonia thought, *I hope I can answer them.* "Well, let's talk. What is worrying you?

"I am not worried. I am not sure that we will be able to stay on the train, if they find out how old we are."

"They won't take us off the train in the middle of nowhere. Remember, Mama said do not talk to strangers. We will just talk to each other. Maybe Arina has a book we can read or a game we can play while on the train. What else worries you?"

"When we get off the train, how will we get to Esther's house?"

"I was told by Leon there are carriages at the station that will take you where you want to go. I am to give him the paper with Esther's address. He will take us there."

"I hope the house is as nice as Rada's."

Sonia said to herself, *I am hoping all goes like we planned.* "Anna, I am sleepy. Good night. Love you."

"Me too. Good night."

45

Gifts for the Family

SONIA WAS UP AND DRESSED when their morning visitor arrived.

Aart asked, "Could I wake Anna? I want to give her a drawing I made for her."

"All right, but don't shake her."

"Anna, Anna, wake up."

"Good morning, Aart. I will miss your wake-up calls."

"Anna, get up. We have a few things we must do today. Aart and I will go downstairs so you can get dressed."

"Wait, I want to give Anna the picture I drew for her."

"Thank you, Aart. It is beautiful. I will put it in my valise."

The girls had a fast breakfast. They asked if they could go into the Lipscani area.

Anna said, "We want to buy Aart and Arina a gift. Can we go ourselves?"

"Do you remember the way? Let us do this. We will go with you. You will lead the way. I will take Aart and Arina with me to buy them shoes. You can go your way. That will be fine with us."

As we approached the main street in the town of Lipscani, Sonia said, "We will meet in two hours right here."

Off went the girls, alone for the first time, shopping.

"Let's go for Arina's and Aart's gifts first."

Within a short time, they purchased a stuffed dog for Aart. Anna found a lovely bracelet for Arina. They were off to the hat shop.

The shopkeeper asked, "Weren't you the young ladies who were here last week?"

"Yes," said Anna. "We are here to purchase a men's cap as well as a ladies' hat as gifts. Can we see men's caps please?"

The shopkeeper was delighted to see the young ladies again since they were purchasing items.

"I have just the one cap called a gentlemen's cap. The tag reads a traditional wool blend tweed made from 75 percent wool and 25 percent other materials. It is fully lined."

"Yes, it is just what we wanted. We will take it. Now a ladies' hat please. We would like to see something colorful that fits tight."

"I have just the hat. This red wool cap brings a flair to a classic style. Decorative gathers at the seams, and between the gathers is a dynamic rose waiting to be admired. The fitted top flares out into a small perky brim, giving a traditional cloche look."

Sonia fell in love with this hat. She asked, "May I try it on?"

"Definitely," said the shopkeeper.

"Sonia, you look beautiful in that hat." Anna then asked, "May I try on a hat?"

The girls had a wonderful hour trying on hats.

Sonia announced, "We will take both the cap and the hat. Could you wrap them for us? They are gifts."

As the girls walked back to their meeting place with their packages, Anna said, "What a grand day. When we get to Bucharest, let's go shopping again. This was fun."

They both started giggling. When the girls approached the meeting place, they saw everyone waiting for them.

Anna asked, "Are we late?"

Rada replied, "Just on time."

While walking to Rada's house, Aart was tell the girls the exciting day he had. When they reached the house, the girls hurriedly put their packages in the bedroom. They came down the stairs to help with dinner.

"Rada, can we help you?"

"Yes, Anna. Would you help Arina set the table? Sonia, would you cut the black bread I bought from the baker? Be careful. The bread is hot."

"Do they have shopping areas in Bucharest?"

Rada replied with a giggle. "I hope so…I have never been there, so I really cannot say."

Leon entered the house. His children were the first to greet him. They started by telling him what a wonderful day they had.

Leon then asked the girls, "How was your day?"

Anna said, "Can we tell you after dinner about our day?"

They were all hungry. There was no conversation during dinner. Everyone helped to clear the table, then went into the sitting room.

The girls said, "Excuse us. We will be down shortly."

To everyone's surprise, they quickly entered the sitting room with packages.

Aart asked, "What do you have in those packages?"

"Anna and I are so grateful for your kindness. We decided to give thank-you gifts. I guess, Aart, you are first. We hope you like it."

Anna handed him the package. He did not wait to sit down. He tore the wrapper, then opened the box. Out popped this stuffed dog.

"Thank you. I always wanted a dog in bed with me."

"Arina, your package is smaller, but we hope you like it."

Anna handed her the box. Arina was slower in opening the wrapping.

"How did you know I wanted a charm bracelet?" She ran and hugged the girls. "Thank you. Can I wear it now?"

Sonia replied, "Definitely. It is yours. Leon, you are next."

Anna handed him a box.

"I really appreciate this. I did not do anything."

"You allowed us to be in your home. We appreciate that."

He started to tear the wrapper. The box fell open; the cap fell out.

"Wow, this is dandy. I am going to try it on now. How do I look?"

"You look like an English country gentleman."

"Girls, thank you. I always wanted a cap like this."

Anna handed Rada her wrapped gift box.

Rada said, "It is wrapped so beautifully. I may not want to open it."

"We hope you like this. We did not know what to expect when we saw the red scarf waving at us on that icy river. We never expected to be treated like family. We are extremely grateful. This is the least we could do to say thank you."

Anna gave her the box. Rada tore open the wrapper and opened the lid. She gave a gasp as she pulled out the red hat. A tear appeared in the corner of her eye.

"Girls, this is beautiful. I must try this on now."

"Yes," Anna said, "or Sonia will take it away from you."

They all laughed. Rada put on the hat.

Leon said, "Rada, you look beautiful."

"Thank you, Leon. I must go to the looking glass to see for myself. Girls, it is a beautiful gift. Thank you so much."

Everyone was pleased with their presents.

Leon asked, "Would you like to hear a short story?"

They all enjoyed the amusing story. The girls said good night, then went upstairs.

Anna said, "Let's pack so we will not have to rush tomorrow. I have so much to ask you."

"Let's pack first, then I will answer all your questions if I can."

"When we are on the train, if someone sits next to me, what should I do?"

"Leon explained how the train seats are arranged in the overnight trains. We have two seats facing each other. No one else can sit there. Anna, we have food, drinks, a blanket, and our own seat. Please stop worrying about the train. I do not know about a bathroom. We will ask Rada. Do not pack your toothbrush or hairbrush. You will still need them. Let's go to sleep. We may not get much sleep on the train."

"Sonia, do you mind if I sleep with you tonight?"

"Just bring your own pillow."

Anna grabbed her pillow. She scrambled into bed with Sonia. Within minutes, she fell fast asleep. Sonia was having a hard time sleeping. She was thinking of Bucharest. *What will the house be like? Will Esther and her daughter Sonya be friendly? What is happening in Hajsyn?* She finally fell asleep.

Leaving Moldova

WHEN SONIA, AWOKE IT WAS still dark. She was still thinking of home. She missed her Mama and Papa. She understood why they had to leave. She promised herself that one day, they were going to bring their family to America. She wondered about Boris. Why was he so nice to them? Why did he and his sister help us? *When I am able to, I will ask Rada. They are lovely people. I am glad we met them.*

The daylight started coming through the window. Sonia completed packing, remembering to leave her toothbrush and hairbrush out of the valise. Anna was waking up.

"Get up, sleepyhead. I have finished packing. Let's get you packed. Anna, the extra money you have after shopping, put into your pouch with the gold necklace."

The girls cleaned up the room, then proceeded down the stairs.

Aart was about to climb the stairs when he saw Anna at the top. He said, "Did you eat breakfast?"

"No, but I am going to eat now."

"I will be waiting for you outside."

The girls finished breakfast. They went outside to play a game. They drew boxes on the ground, then threw stones in the boxes. They then jumped on one foot to retrieve the stones. Sonia found a blue-green stone on the sidewalk. She decided to keep this as a remembrance.

Arina said, "I have a box full of stones."

"I would like to keep this one. I like the colors."

The girls had just started to play the game when Leon came walking up the street.

"Does Mommy know you are home?"

"Yes, she and I decided this last night. We thought we would go to the train station with Sonia and Anna."

Aart said, "That would be fun, Papa. When do we leave?"

"In a while. I first want to talk to both of you. Anna and Sonia, please come too. Rada, I am home," Leon shouted. "I will be with the children."

"Anna and Sonia, please come upstairs. I want to make sure you packed everything. We leave no later than 4:00 p.m."

"Okay," Leon agreed.

Leon sat the children down. He wanted to explain why their mother was going on the train with the girls. Leon started by saying, "Sonia and Anna have never been on a train. Mommy is going with them for the first train ride. They will be stopping in a small town near Lipscani. Mommy and the girls will have to get off this train. There is a second train that will take the girls to Bucharest. The problem is, that next train will not be coming into the station for five hours. Mommy and I decided that she should stay with the girls until this next train arrives. She wants to make sure they get on the correct train. Mommy will take the next train back home. She will be home late tonight."

"That is wonderful idea," said Aart. "We have never seen a real train. Can we go on the train?"

"No, you must have a ticket. Maybe someday, but not today. Mommy packed supper. We will eat in the station."

Rada came down the stairs with the girls, Anna with her new valise, Sonia holding hers. Everyone reached for their coats. Leon took the packages, and off they went.

The Train to the Border Crossing

THE STATION WAS WITHIN A fifteen-minute walk. Aart was lagging behind. Leon ended up carrying him. They reached the station and found an empty bench. Just as a train was pulling in, it made a loud screeching sound. That made Aart jump into Leon's lap. He hid his face in Leon's shoulder. Arina held both hands over her ears.

"It is okay, children. All trains make a noise like that when they come into the station. That is how they stop."

"Daddy, I don't think I want to go on a train," said Aart.

Everyone laughed.

Sonia said to Rada, "Thank you for coming with us."

Rada, Anna, and Sonia entered the station master's room.

Sonia asked, "To whom do we present our travel papers?"

The station master replied, "I will take them. Please sit here until I process and stamp them."

Sonia thought it seemed like a long time since the station master left. Sonia was getting nervous. Finally, he returned.

He addressed Rada. "Are you the adult traveling with the girls?"

"Yes."

The station master then asked, "Who is Sonia? Who is Anna? Well, ladies, have a good trip." He turned to Rada. "May I see your papers?"

"I am a citizen of Moldova. Here are my papers."

"I just needed to check the date. You are clear to go. Have a good trip."

Rada took the girls to the area where Leon was sitting with the children.

Leon asked, "All finished?"

"Yes, now we can eat."

"Remember, Aart, when the train comes in, it will make the same loud noise. So do not get frightened."

"Okay, Papa. But can I sit next to you?"

"Yes."

Anna said, "You can sit next to me as well." Aart grabbed her hand.

The time went by quickly. Their train was approaching. The station master called, "Train number 677 approaching track 3. All boarding in ten minutes."

Leon said, "Let's say our goodbyes now."

Aart grabbed Anna's hand again. "I will miss you." He started to cry.

Arina said, "Sonia, write so I will have your address. I promise I will answer." She hugged both girls.

"We must be on the train."

Leon kissed both girls on the cheek. He said, "Have a good life." They turned and left the station.

Rada helped the girls onto the train. She found their seats.

Anna said, "Sonia, you were right. We have separate seats just for us."

Rada said, "Do not get too comfortable. We will be getting off in a little while. Keep your bags close. Are you excited about going to Bucharest?"

"A little frightened and excited for we will be on our own. My mother's sister has a friend who has daughter that is about my age. Her name is Sonya. That should be interesting."

"Sonia, what are you going to do in Bucharest?"

"I want to go to school. I must learn English so when I get to America, I want to be speaking the language."

"Sonia, that is a very adult attitude."

"Anna will have to go to school. She is underage."

The conductor came to our car. He shouted, "Ungheni Prut change here for the train to Bucharest."

Rada said, "Stay seated for the train makes a sudden movement. You can fall."

It took a while for the train to make a complete stop. They began to allow passengers off. They waited till most of the people left the car.

Rada said, "We can go to the door."

The conductor helped the girls down the steps. He then handed them their valises.

A conductor announced, "The train to Bucharest is coming in on this track. All passengers can stay in this area."

"Anna and I need to go potty."

Rada said, "They have a few closets at the end of the platform."

Sonia questioned, "Closets?"

Rada explained, "That is a room with a stationary toilet that has water that flushes down the waste."

Anna said, "Let's go. I must see this."

Both girls were gone for some time. They finally returned.

Sonia explained, "I really had to pull Anna away. She kept on pulling on the cord to watch the water go down the bowl."

They sat on a bench and put their valises on the bench as well. Anna lay down on her coat. She fell fast asleep on the bench. Her coat was under her.

Mystery Solved

SONIA THOUGHT NOW WOULD BE a good time to question Rada.

"Rada, did you always live in Moldova?"

"No, I was raised in Ukraine, not too far from where you lived. When I got married, I moved to Moldova. Leon was employed with the bank when I married him. Boris stayed behind. He still lives in our mother's house."

"Do you mind if I ask you a few questions?"

"No. I have some questions too I hope you can answer, Sonia."

"Before I ask my question, I want to thank you again for making us feel like part of your family. We appreciate all the help you have given us, especially your brother. We know he is the constable of the community. Anna and I were frightened of him at first. We thought if our father trusted him, we should also. Being with him, we realized he is a caring person like you."

"Boris was always a kind, caring person. This job has changed him. I was wondering, Sonia. There had to be a connection between someone in your family and Boris." Rada said, "I remembered when Boris was a boy, around nine years old, he fell in the school grounds. No one would help him. One young man about his age came to help him. He was kind to Boris. He gathered his scattered school books and cleaned his scraped bleeding knee.

"What is your father's name?"

"Avraham, yes."

"Did he go to school or just to religious school?"

"My father had to go to both. His father had a general store. He had to learn both languages."

"Do you know your father's age?"

"He is thirty-one. How old is Boris?"

55

"Thirty-one. I think we found the connection. Boris spoke about Avraham all the time. They became best friends. They did everything together. One day, Boris came home. He announced, 'Avraham and I are blood brothers. We cut our fingers. We then put the bloody fingers together. This makes us blood brothers for life.' My mother was horrified. She said, 'You cannot see your friend again. He is Jewish. The new law does not allow being friends with Jews.' My father said, "When you are out of school this summer, you will go to the army.' That was the last time I remember Boris saying anything about Avraham."

Sonia was careful with what she said now. She did not want any trouble for Boris or her father.

"The only thing I know is Boris comes to the store when he needs supplies for himself or the soldiers. They never seemed friendly when Boris is in the store. My father said to the boys, 'Boris is the constable of this community. Always show him respect.'"

Sonia was thinking, *No wonder Boris took us away. I know now why my parents trusted their daughters with him.*

Both of them were thinking their own thoughts when Rada said, "Sonia, I promise you I will not say anything to Leon or Boris about this friendship."

"Neither will I even mention it to Anna."

"Thank you, Rada, for helping solve this puzzle."

"Thank you, Sonia." And they both laughed.

Anna was just waking up when the conductor said, "The train for Bucharest is on time."

Rada asked, "Are you girls hungry? Maybe you should have dinner now. There would be less food to carry."

Anna said, "Good idea. I am always hungry."

They finished eating and cleaning up as the train was just pulling into the station.

"Girls, go to the closet while I am here. Anna, do not play with the cord."

The Train to Bucharest

THE TRAIN HAD JUST PULLED into the station. The station master said, "All aboard." He announced he would be taking tickets upon boarding. Rada gave the tickets to the station master. He stamped and returned them. The conductor helped the girls on to the train. Rada then boarded the train. Sonia found their seats. She got Anna seated next to the window. Sonia sat across from her. Rada then handed the stamped tickets to Sonia.

"You keep these in your coat pocket. The conductor may want to see them again. If he asks about your adult, say, 'She put us on the train. Our aunt is meeting us.' He may ask to see your tickets again. Just make sure he gives them back to you. I know you will not be asked again, but do not get upset if he does. They sometimes check. Just remember this train only stops in Bucharest." Rada hesitated for a minute but knew she had to get off the train. "Girls, if you ever need help, let us know. We will be there for you."

"Thank you, Rada. You are a good friend."

"Have a good life, girls. Let us know where you are. Write so we know how you are doing."

"We promise."

Rada turned and left the train.

The conductor yelled, "All aboard."

The train gave a lurch and started off. Anna grabbed Sonia's arm. She held it tight.

"Anna, please, you are hurting me. Everything is going to be fine. We are going to Bucharest, then America. Why don't you start writing a letter to Rada? Maybe draw a picture."

The motion of the train put both girls to sleep. Anna woke up. She shook Sonia. "Wake up. Are we there yet?"

"Anna, when you see daylight, we will be close to Bucharest. The conductor will announce when we are close."

"Sonia, are you hungry?"

"Are you telling me you are hungry, Anna?"

"Yes."

"Let's see what is in the bag. Would you like hard-boiled eggs, black bread with jam? There is tea in a jar. We also have cookies."

"That would be fine, Sonia. What will you have?"

"There is another bag. It has the exact same thing. Let's eat."

"Do you know where the closets are?"

"No. I will find out. There is a lady sitting across from us. After we finish our snack, I will ask her where the toilets are in this car."

"Sonia, please ask that lady. I have to go."

"Okay, you just sit still. Excuse me. Could you tell me where the toilets are in this compartment?"

"Oh, sweetie, definitely. They are at the end of this car. I will show your sister. I have to use it myself."

Off went Anna with the stranger. Anna returned faster than Sonia expected. The stranger followed shortly after.

"Anna, are you okay?"

"Yes, the toilets are the same as in the station."

Sonia laughed. She then took out a game, follow the dots. They played till all the boxes got filled.

Anna enjoyed looking out the window. She enjoyed seeing the animals roaming. After a while, Anna took out a book to read. Sonia opened a book that teaches English. While they were in the bookstore in Lipscani, she purchased it.

The train made no stops. The girls did not have anyone ask them for their papers. The conductor came into their car. He announced, "Bucharest in one hour." He then proceeded into the next car.

The girls were getting excited.

"Sonia, why don't you ask that nice lady where would the carriages be when we get off the train."

Sonia walked across the aisle. "May I ask you a question?"

"Of course," the woman replied.

"When we leave the train station, where would we find the carriages to take us to our aunt's house?"

"Just follow me. I am going there as well."

"Thank you."

"Anna, we are going to follow that lady. She is going there as well. It will look like we are with her, so no one will question us."

The girls made a quick trip to the toilets, then packed their belongings into their valises.

Finally, the conductor came through their car announcing, "Bucharest in ten minutes. Stay in your seats until the train stops."

They watched as the train entered the station. It slowed down till it met the platform, then stopped.

The lady said, "Wait until the crowd gets off. They get rather pushy."

They waited till the passengers left the car, then started walking to the door. The conductor was there to help all of them down the steps and on to the platform. Anna and Sonia walked with the lady through the station doors as though they belonged with her. In the street before them were many horse-drawn carriages.

Sonia said, "Thank you for your help."

"Girls, my name is Dora. Let me give you my calling card in case you need help."

The card reads "Dora Farkat, Soseaua Kiseleff 18."

"I am Sonia Zitefsky. This is my sister Anna Zitefsky. We are visiting our aunt on our way to America."

"How exciting."

They accepted Dora's card, then gave her their address. Dora hailed a carriage for them. She told the driver to take them to Calia Victoriei Blvd 9. The girls thanked Dora. They were helped into the carriage and were on their way.

The Letters Home

BACK IN HAJSYN, LIFE SETTLED into the same routine. Avraham was helping customers; Raisa was restocking the shelves. Both were anxiously waiting to hear from Boris. They were concerned about the girls. They had not heard from them since they left.

This particular Saturday, Sol and Lou were brushing the horses in the barn when they spotted Boris coming down the road driving the two horses with the wagon attached. He pulled up in front of the store. He proceeded inside. Avraham was pleased to see him.

"Good morning, Constable. What can I do for you today?"

"One of my wheels seem to be wobbling. My horse also needs a new bit. This one is broken."

Avraham called the boys. He told them to take the horses and wagon in the barn. They were to unhook the horses, then put the wagon in the first stall.

"The constable and I must go to the barn. I will see what can be done about the bit. Raisa, would you help the patrons while I see to the constable's needs."

Avraham and Boris left the shop. Avraham was so anxious to know about the girls. While walking toward the barn, Avraham said, "It is a beautiful day. Boris, how is your day?"

Boris replied, "It is the most beautiful day."

In the barn, Boris gave Avraham three letters—one from Sonia, the second from Anna, the third from Rada.

Avraham asked, "Why would Rada be writing to us?"

"Read it, and you will see."

"I will read Rada's now. The girls' letters will be read when we get in the house. We informed the boys the girls are alive. We explained why we had to send them away. They were so moved they started to cry."

Boris handed the three letters to Avraham. He opened Rada's letter. He read it aloud, letting Boris hear what Rada has written.

"After you read them, burn them."

"Did you read this?"

"Yes."

Dear Mr. and Mrs. Zitefsky,

I have just put Sonia and Anna on the train to Bucharest. They will reach Bucharest in twenty hours. They are well and excited. This is the first time they are really alone. They stayed with my family until the border crossing papers were completed. I must tell you my husband and I have grown quite fond of your daughters. We were reluctant to see them leave. Our four-year-old son is in love with Anna. I would have no concern about your girls. Sonia handles herself as though she were eighteen. They will be fine. They were told if they need anything, just write to us. We would help them. We cashed the gold coins. We purchased a valise for Anna. The girls bought clothes they needed. I purchased the train tickets. I also changed some coins into Romanian coins. This will pay for the carriage ride to your friend's house. They need some spending money. I thank you for the gold coins you sent me. I feel I should send them back. Your girls are now a part of our family.

Sincerely, Rada

Avraham looked toward Boris. "I am forever in your debt. There are no words that could tell you how grateful we are."

"Avraham, I had a wonderful time with your daughters. Anna has a beautiful singing voice. Sonia is just beautiful and smart. She knows what she wants. She takes care of Anna like a mother. We sang songs while traveling in the wagon as well as walking across the icy river. They never complained about the conditions."

"Boris, you are a smart one. When you said you would not tell me any more of your plans, I was taken aback when the commandant told me they found a boot in a larger hole in the ice further up the river. Truly, my friend, I was in shock."

"Avraham, I knew they would not question you any further when he saw your face."

"Truly, my friend, I was shocked."

"Boris, what happened to Anna's valise?"

"It is in your barn. I had to carry Anna across the river. Water settled on top of the ice, making it difficult for her to walk with the heavy boots. Sonia fell a few times. She had to carry my skates. I could not carry two valises and Anna."

"Boris, you are truly a good friend."

"No, Avraham. You're brother a blood brother."

Both men left the barn and walked toward the shop. Lou took the horse that belonged to Boris and saddled it up. He then tied it to the post in front of the store. Both men entered the shop. Raisa looked up.

Avraham said, "It is a beautiful day."

Boris purchased the bit. He then left the shop.

The day went by slowly for Raisa. She so much wanted to read the girls' letters.

Avraham said, "Boys, we are closing early today. Mama cannot stand on her feet much longer. Put the closed sign on the door."

Within a half hour, the store was closed. As they all walked toward the house, Sol asked, "Did Boris bring letters from the girls?"

"Yes, that is why we closed early. Mama and I wanted to read those letters."

The family settled in the sitting room. Avraham started to read.

Dear Mama and Papa,

I did not want to waste time in sending you this letter. We knew you and Papa were worried. Anna and I are writing you while we are on the train to Bucharest. We have to send our letters to Rada. She will post them to Boris for you. Boris was just wonderful. He made sure we were safe. He was careful that we crossed the icy river safely. We met his sister in the middle of the river. She took us to her home. We lived with her family till our travel papers were ready. His sister Rada was just amazing. She helped us with all the money exchange and shopping. I have so much to tell you, but I want this letter to get to you, so I am making it short. We are fine. I promise to write a long letter and tell you all about our experiences. We love you. We promise to see the family in America. Say hello to Sol and Lou. We miss them.

Love, Sonia

Dear Rada,

Just a short note. We are still on the train, but we wanted these attached letters you are to receive to go to our parents. We know they are worried. Could you please forward? I will send a long letter when we get to our new house. Thank you again.

Love, Sonia and Anna

Dear Mama and Papa,

Sonia and I are on the train to Bucharest. It is called an overnight train. We have our own seat to sleep in. We do bounce around a bit. We lived with Boris's sister in her house of red bricks. They have a toilet inside the house. It had a long chain attached to the inside. Every time you went to the bathroom, you pulled the chain. Water came to the bowl to wash—Sonia, how do I say poop? Wash your waste away. The train also has the same toilets. I will write later and tell you all the new places we saw. Sonia and I are fine. We will be leaving the train soon. I have to close this letter. Love to the boys, you, and Papa.

Sol said, "It seems that the girls had quite a trip. How did they go across the river?"

Avraham answered, "They wore rubber boots. Anna rode on Boris's back. She had trouble walking in the boots. Boris had to carry her across."

"Mama said there were three letters. Who wrote the third one?"

"Boris's sister, Rada. I will show it to you later. I am hungry. Let's eat."

The big discussion at dinner was the toilet that Anna wrote about.

Lou said, "I bet there is no smell like the outhouse."

Sol said, "Where do they get the water? Where does it go when you are finished? Write to Anna and ask her."

"Boys, remember, do not tell anyone about these letters from the girls. We will all be in trouble."

"Papa, don't worry. We will not say a word."

After the boys went to bed, Avraham gave Raisa the letter that Rada wrote.

After she finished reading the letter, Raisa said, "I miss the girls." She started to cry.

Avraham took Raisa in his arms and whispered in her ear, "I know you are carrying a little girl. I am naming her Reba after your mother."

Raisa stopped crying. She kissed Avraham. "You always know the right thing to say that will stop me from crying."

"Let's go to bed, Raisa. We had a very emotional day."

PART 3

The Carriage Ride

THE DRIVER TOOK THEIR VALISES and helped them into the carriage. The girls settled themselves comfortably.

Anna asked, "Do you know where we are going?"

"No, I cannot converse with him. I will show him the paper with Esther's address. Dora only told him where we were going."

At that moment, the carriage driver turned his head.

He said to the girls in Yiddish. "Ich bin a yed-ich farshtast Yiddish." I am Jewish. I understand Yiddish.

Sonia responded in Yiddish, "Mein syaster un ich farshtast Yiddish." My sister and I speak and understand Yiddish. "De vais veu de geyst?" Do you know where Calia Victoriei Blvd 9 is located?

The driver laughed. He responded, "Ich vais vue ich geyt." I know where I am going.

Sonia asked, "Tis izoi hayzer vayt fun du?"

The driver responded, "Ve vill kimmin tu da hayzer un finif menute." We will be at the house in five minutes. "Ver geyst du zayn?" Who are you going to see?

"Mer geyt zayan mein tanta." We are visiting our aunt.

"Don tanta hutt au shansta hayzer." Your aunt lives in a beautiful house.

Anna said to Sonia, "He thinks we are going to our aunt's house."

"I know. We will probably never see him again, so why brother to correct him."

As the girls conversed in Ukrainian, the driver stopped the carriage. He helped the girls out, then handed them their valise.

The driver said in Yiddish, "Your friend paid your fare."

"Dunka shane," said Sonia. Both girls proceeded to the front door.

Arriving at Calia Victoriei Blvd 9, Bucharest

SONIA TUGGED THE DOOR PULL.

"Anna, are you feeling well? You look pale."

"I am fine."

Sonia proceeded to tug at the door pull again. The door opened. A young girl about the same age as Sonia opened the door. The young girl jumped. She hugged Sonia as well as Anna.

"We have been expecting you all morning. Mama, Mama, hurry. The girls are here."

Esther came from the back of the house, wiping her hands with the bottom of her apron. "I am so happy to see you. I was getting worried. Your train pulled in two hours ago. We thought you would be here earlier."

Esther started to walk toward the girls. Sonia extended her hand.

"My name is Sonia Zitefsky. This is my sister, Anna Zitefsky. My mother told me you are a good friend of my aunt Pessy in America."

"Yes, we went to school together in Hajsyn. Your aunt stayed here with her two boys on her way to America. Her husband sent for her. Girls, we are so pleased you are here. Please make this your home while you are in Bucharest. Can I get you something to eat or drink?"

Anna answered, "Yes, please, something to drink."

"And you, Sonia?"

"The same please."

Sonya asked, "How was the train ride? You must be tired? Did you sleep?"

"Yes, the movement of the train rocked us to sleep."

Esther returned with a tray of cookies and drinks.

"Here we are, girls. Sonya, there are cookies for you as well. Ladies, I must go back to start dinner. Sonya, why don't you show the girls around the house. Their room is on the third floor. Girls, I cannot wait for you to meet the people who live here."

Sonia asked as she munched on a cookie, "How many people live in this house?"

"Our guests live here year-round. They consider this their home. They all have their meals here," she said as they passed the dining room. "We are like one large family. You and Anna will meet them tonight at dinner."

Sonia asked, "Could we see where we will be living? We would like to put our valises somewhere. Anna, are you finished?"

"Yes."

Sonya went on to say, "The family lives on the third floor. All guests live on the second floor. Come, the stairs are at the end of this hallway."

They walked up a large winding staircase to the second floor. They walked down a hallway to another staircase, not quite as fancy as the first. There was a long hallway on the third floor that went from one end of the house to the other end.

Sonya said, "Your room is in the back of the house."

When the girls entered their room, they were pleasantly surprised. This was a lovely extra-large room with two beds, a table, and two sitting chairs for reading. There was a desk to use for school. There were drawers to hold paper for letter writing.

"This is very nice. Where do we go to—"

Before Anna could finish her sentence, Sonya said as she opened the door, "The salon is here."

This room had a beautiful white toilet, a deep stationary white tub, and a white sink.

Anna asked, "Is this all for us?"

"Yes, my mother thought you may be here for a while. The two of you would want some privacy."

Anna said, "Thank you. That was very sweet of both of you."

Sonia asked, "Would you mind if we unpacked and washed before we go down for dinner?"

"Not at all. I will see you at dinner. My mother rings a bell. This will let you know dinner is ready. You will meet the other renters at dinner."

Both girls thanked Sonya. She then left their room.

"What a lovely room. We have our own bath and toilet room."

Sonia corrected her, "Anna, it is called a salon."

Anna said, "I wonder if it works the same way as the one in the train station."

Sonia laughed. "Go see for yourself, but only flush once please. We have unpacking to do."

"Sonia, what do you think we should do on our first day in Bucharest?"

"First, we should get acquainted with the area. We must learn the streets so we know where we are going. We have to know where we live. We have to know how to get back to the house. I think we should write the address of where we are living on a piece of paper. Let's keep this with us at all times. If we get lost, we can ask someone how to get back to this address."

"That's a good idea."

"I will ask Sonya if she would go with us for a few days so we can get familiar with the area. Maybe next week we can venture a little further out ourselves. We will have to find a school for you. I have to find a school that teaches me English and French."

"Sonia, do you think they will have a street with shops on it?"

"I think they do. This looks like a big city. I think we have other things to do first."

"Let's hurry. We have to get ready. We have to go downstairs to meet the other tenants."

"What are you going to wear, Anna?"

"I thought the pink dress with the pleated skirt."

"Oh, that's good. You look very pretty in that dress."

"Sonia, how about you?"

"I was considering the purple top and a white skirt."

"No. Please, you must wear something blue to match your eyes."

"All right, the blue jacket with the white skirt."

"Yes, that will be beautiful."

"We must hurry. Esther rings the bell at exactly six o'clock. We cannot be late. Turn around, Anna. I will button up your back."

"Thank you."

They opened up the bedroom door and met Sonya at the top of the stairs as the dong-dong went off.

Sonia asked, "Is everyone so prompt?"

"No." Sonya laughed. "Only when we have important guests."

"Really! Who?"

"The two of you."

They all laughed.

Meeting the Bucharest Family

THE THREE GIRLS WALKED INTO the dining room. The men rose from their seats.

Esther said, "May I introduce Anna Zitefsky and her sister Sonia Zitefsky. They are our new guests. They will be living here for a while. They are on their way to America. Girls, this is Rabbi Morris Rosen and his wife, Faygie. He is a rabbi at the great Polish synagogue. This is Antoine Durant. He teaches at the University of Bucharest. The last person in our family is Yankel Levy. He is an actor and manager at the Yiddish theatre a few blocks from us. Now that we have all been introduced, let's eat."

Two women started carrying out trays of food. They placed the trays on the center of the table.

Easter announced, "Help yourselves. If you need help, ladies, we will help you. Sometimes the trays are heavy."

The next minute, everyone started talking at once. The rabbi was the first to ask the girls, "Where are you from?"

Sonia answered, "We are from a small village called Hajsyn in Ukraine."

Yankel asked, "Do you have any brothers or sisters?"

Anna answered, "Yes, we have two brothers who go to school and work in our father's general store. There is only one general store in this small village."

"What is a general store?" asked Faygie.

"It is a store that sells groceries, supplies, and other sundry items. It was started by our great-grandfather, passed on to our grandfather, then passed on to our father. Times are bad in Ukraine at this time. There are pogroms. The soldiers are killing the Jewish people. When Anna and I live in America, we are going to work. We will make enough money to send for our family to come to America."

Yankel said, "That's a pretty big order for two small girls."

"We will be living with our mother's sister and go to work."

Antoine said, "Come to the university. You can learn to be a teacher."

"Thank you," Sonia said. "I will look into that."

Rabbi Rosen asked, "Do you know Hebrew?"

"In our village, girls were not invited to go to Hebrew school. That was only for boys."

Anna said, "Our father taught us Hebrew."

Rabbi then asked, "Would you like to go to services this Saturday morning?"

Anna answered quickly, "Yes."

Esther interrupted the conversation, "The food is getting cold."

The platters were passed around. Yankel held the platters, giving Anna the opportunity to choose what she wanted off the platter. Sonia was helped by Antoine. The dinner went smoothly. The servers asked if the diners wanted chocolate or lemon cake with a cup of tea.

Both girls said, "Chocolate cake please and a cup of tea."

Dessert was served and consumed. The rabbi and his wife excused themselves and went for a walk. Sonia asked Sonya if she could sit with them. The girls had questions, hoping she could answer some of them. Yankel and Antoine overheard the girls. They interrupted.

"Maybe we could help."

Sonia said, "Definitely. Please join us. We need to find a school for Anna. She had one more year to finish school in Ukraine. We would like Anna to speak English before we go to America."

Antoine said, "What a good idea. I will ask at the university. One professor must know of a free secondary school that gives language courses."

Anna said, "Thank you, Antoine."

Sonia asked if the university offered French and English courses. Antoine offered to see if there were courses that the university offered that included languages.

"Sonia, when I get some information, maybe you can come with me. I will help you with filling out the forms."

"Thank you, Antoine."

Yankel said, "Is there anything else we can help you with?"

"Yes," both girls said. "We do not know our way around Bucharest."

Sonya said, "This Sunday, if we are all free, let's take the girls around Bucharest."

"A great idea," said Yankel.

Sonia said, "In the meantime, we will get lost just going out the front door."

Sonya said, "Tomorrow, I will take you to all the important places. Anna and you will have to know how to find the food shop, the bakery, the apothecary. Of course, you will have to know how to come back home. By the way, here is a house key for each of you. Do not lose it."

"Thank you. Sonya, I do have one question for you. Being we both have the same name, are you called by your Hebrew name?"

"Yes, my mother calls me Sura all the time."

Both Anna and Sonia started to laugh.

Sonia said, "That is my Hebrew name as well."

Sonya said, "This is easy to solve. My mother calls me Sura all the time, so I will be Sura, and you can be Sonia."

Anna said, "I am getting tired. We had a really busy day. Do you mind if Sonia and I go upstairs?"

Everyone agreed.

Both girls said, "Thank you, Sonya, Yankel, and Antoine for a wonderful first evening in Bucharest."

The girls said good night to Esther and thanked her for a wonderful meal.

Sonia asked, "Point us in the right direction please."

Sonya escorted both girls to their door, said good night, and waited for them to enter their room.

Sonia said to Anna, "Do not ask me anything. We will talk tomorrow please."

"Yes," said Anna. "Good night."

"Anna, do not pull the toilet cord more than once please. Good night," whispered Sonia.

Anna had trouble sleeping. She looked over and saw Sonia was fast asleep. She had so many questions swimming around in her head. She got up from bed, paced the floor, and went to the desk. She had to write down her questions. She found a sheet of paper and looked for a writing instrument. She remembered she had one in her purse. She used it when she wrote to her parents. She finally sat at the desk and started writing.

Are there schools within walking distance?

Are there food stores nearby?

Is there a park close by?

What do girls do for fun?

Are there shopping streets?

Are there eating places within walking distance?

Anna suddenly got tired. She left the questions on the desk and decided to go to sleep. She no sooner got into bed, then she fell asleep.

The room was dark, and both girls were fast asleep. A small fly was hovering over Sonia's face, waking her up. She saw Anna was still sleeping. She decided to let her sleep. Sonia got out of bed and walked around the room. She had not really looked around. They rushed to meet the other people who were living there.

If I sent a letter home describing this room, no one would believe me. Rada would. It is beautiful, large, and has the bathing area inside the bedroom. As Sonia walked around, she saw the note on the desk that Anna had written. She said to herself, *Good questions.*

Sonia walked into the bathroom and decided to take a hot bath, that is, if she could find where the water comes from. She finally found the water levers at the top of the tub. She looked to see what holds the water in the tub. She spied a round rubber plug. She inserted the plug in the hole and ran the water. The water was cold. She then turned the second lever that was hot. *Oh my, the two levers will give you water that is great to bathe in.* With this, Sonia stepped into the tub, sat down, and enjoyed the hot water running around her. On the stool next to the tub, she found a bar of soap, a washcloth, and a large towel. There was one for her; one was for Anna. *Wait till Anna sees this. She will be in here all day every day.* Sonia relaxed in the tub for a few minutes, then started to bathe.

Esther must have a lot of money to own a house like this. That reminds me I have to find out how many gold coins we still have. I must get dressed, wake Anna so we can start our day. We do have to find the bank and the banker name that Papa put in my pouch. I remember his name, Solomon Bally, but not sure of the bank. I will check my pouch when I get out of this wonderful tub.

Sonia was not quite sure on what to do now that she wanted to leave the tub. She decided to pull out the plug. As soon as she did that, the water went rushing down the hole. She thought, *Maybe the water is going into the floor below.* She put the plug back into the hole until she could ask Sura how this tub worked.

Exploring Bucharest

SONIA WAS SURPRISED TO FIND Anna still in a deep sleep. She decided to dress and go downstairs. She wanted to explore the house in the daylight. She left a note for Anna.

> I am downstairs. I am waiting for you for breakfast.

Sonia quietly walked out the bedroom door, down the hallway and down one flight of stairs, turned and walked toward the hall and the second flight going to the main floor. She met Antoine at the bottom of the stairs.

"Good morning, Sonia. Did you sleep well?"

"Yes, I fell asleep as soon as I put my head on the pillow. Anna is still sleeping."

"I think we should talk about going to the university," said Antoine. "They do have individual classes for students who are not looking for a diploma. They are trying to fill the classrooms with students who only are interested in being part-time students. I feel you would qualify."

Sonia said, "Yes, that is exactly what I am interested in doing. Thank you for looking up this information for me. I would like to go sometime, when I am better acquainted with my surroundings."

"I understand," said Antoine. "Would you like me to go with you?"

"Yes," responded Sonia.

"I have to tell you there is a small fee if you are not born in Romania. Do you have papers?"

"Yes," said Sonia.

Mostly everyone was seated and having breakfast.

As Sonia and Antoine entered the dining room, Esther asked, "Where is Anna?"

"She is sound asleep. I left her a note telling her I am downstairs. I did not want to wake her."

Rabbi Morris and his wife, Faygie, said, "Good morning, Sonia. How did you sleep?"

"Well, thank you."

"What are your plans for today?" Sonya asked as she entered the room.

"We are going to learn the surrounding area."

Just then, Anna come bouncing into the room. "Good morning, everyone. Thank you for the note, Sonia. Did you eat?"

"No, I waited for you."

Anna sat next to Sonia. She remarked, "What a beautiful table. I have never seen so much food."

Faygie said, "She always does a beautiful table on the weekends. During the week, it's muffins, tea or coffee, and eggs. But today is Friday."

Remarked Sonya, "This was just for you, to say welcome."

"Esther, thank you," said Anna and Sonia. Both girls enjoyed breakfast.

Sonya said, "Sonia and I decided, instead of calling us both Sonya, which will be confusing, we decided that since my mother calls me Sura all the time, I will be called Sura when we are both together. Sonia will remain Sonia. It is really strange we both have the same Yiddish name as well."

Yankel asked, "Sura, where do you want to go first?"

"I feel we should take a walk around the neighborhood. The girls can become familiar with the names of the streets and how to find their way back to the house."

"Great idea."

"Sura, you escort them around. Antoine and I will be at a street corner to test them to see what turn they will take to get back to the house."

This was done for a while. The girls took the test.

Antoine remarked, "They know the streets to get back to the house. Let's take the streetcar going to university Square. We can walk around the park."

Sura asked the girls, "Do you have walking shoes?"

Anna and Sonia started to giggle. Everyone looked at both girls laughing.

Sonia said, "I'm sorry there was an incident that happened. Remembering it made both of us laugh."

Yankel said, "Well, as long it was a good memory."

"We can have lunch at one of the outside cafes."

Sonia said, "Anna and I would love that."

"Maybe we could go inside the university. They may have literature on the courses they give. We may even find out when school starts."

"That would be helpful. Anna must get enrolled in a school before classes start."

Yankel said, "There is a great school near the theatre called Saint Sava National College. It is one of the most prestigious schools in Romania. It is free if you are a Romanian citizen. I have no idea what it costs for noncitizens. I will find out and let you know."

Anna said, "Thank you, Yankel."

Sonia asked, "Is this a Catholic school?"

Antoine said, "No, not religious at all. Sura, hurry up. Here comes a streetcar."

The streetcar stopped to let passengers off. The driver then said, "You may come on now."

The boys helped the girls up the few steps. Yankel moved to the back of the car for there was a long seat in the back. They all piled into this seat. Antoine paid the fare. He joined them in the back of the car.

Anna asked, "What do you call this vehicle?"

Antoine said, "We call it a streetcar. Some call it a trolley. It serves the same purpose to take people from one place to another."

Anna whispered to Sonia, "Sol and Lou would never believe this."

It was a beautiful day. Everyone was enjoying the ride. The girls kept looking at all the houses with their lovely gardens.

The driver announced, "Last stop, University Square. I turn around here to go back."

Everyone got off the horse-drawn streetcar and went their separate ways. Antoine started to tell them about University Square and the university. He pointed out the interesting shops, including the bookstore that was in the square.

He told them, "Everyone buys their books for school at this bookstore."

They started walking toward the university through a park. They noticed on the path to the university, people were in separate stalls selling items, some were used schoolbooks, some shoes, some hats, and some supplies that a student would use in school.

Antoine said, "Come on, there is more to see."

They walked the entire east side of the park till they came to a stall that was selling ice cream. Yankel suggested they stop and have some ice cream instead of eating a meal.

Sonia asked, "What is ice cream?"

Sura was shocked that the girls did not know about ice cream.

Yankel said, "Come, I will treat everyone to this delicious treat."

Anna asked, "How do we eat this?"

Antoine said, "Very fast, or it will melt."

Sura said, "This is a sweet and cold treat. It can be eaten as a dessert or as a treat any time of day."

"Anna," Yankel asked, "what flavor would you like, vanilla or chocolate?"

"We have a selection?"

"Of course."

Anna said, "I want chocolate."

Sonia said, "So do I."

Yankel said to the vendor, "Two chocolate plates please. Sura, what flavor would you like?"

"The same please."

"One more chocolate. Antoine, what flavor would you like?"

"Vanilla."

"Two vanilla plates."

The vendor said, "That will be fifty forint for five plates. Thank you."

The group finished their treat quickly. They started the walking tour again. They stopped at a bookstand. They examined the books on sale. They went into the bookstore.

Anna asked, "What is the difference between the outside stand and the store?"

Sura explained, "The bookstore sells new books. The vendor stand sells used books, for example. Anna, when you start school, you will need certain books. The bookstore will sell it for one price. The vendor will sell it for half the price. It is less money for it was used before. The student then saves money."

"We never had anything like this in Hajsyn."

Anna said, "I feel we should come back here to get walking shoes. My feet are beginning to hurt."

"I agree with that," said Sonia.

The group spent another hour walking in the University Square.

Antoine said to Sonia, "Are you ready to go back?"

Anna answered, "Yes."

They grabbed the first horse-drawn streetcar. Sura went to the back of the streetcar to look for seats. There were seats for all to sit.

Sura said, "Sonia, you are going to direct us home. Anna, you are going to tell us when we have to leave the streetcar."

"I agree with that. This will be a test."

"Let's see," said Anna. "There is a large red dome on a building in the street where we get off. There it is. We get off at the next stop."

"Good," said Sura. "Sonia, you will take us home."

They all got off the streetcar.

Sonia said, "We go down to the big tree, then turn right on the wooden street. We live on that street."

"Wonderful. You both can venture out on your own."

The group entered the house.

The girls said, "We had a wonderful day. Thank you for the ice cream."

"We will see you at dinner."

"Anna, I am going upstairs. Are you coming? I have something to show you."

"Yes, I will be up shortly."

Sonia started up the stairs. Anna went out the front door to pick up the local Yiddish newspaper. It was called the *Jewish Press*. As she was about to turn to enter the house, a good-looking very tall young man passed the house. He turned toward her and smiled. She returned the smile and went into the house. Anna walked into the bedroom.

She asked, "What do you want to show me?"

"Come into the salon. Have you tried the bathtub?"

"Is that what it is called?"

"Yes," said Sonia. "I took a bath this morning, and it was wonderful. Come, I will show you how to fill it."

"Not now, Sonia, I want to read the paper and see if they advertise schools. Sura said they might have some in this newspaper."

"I will write a letter to Rada in the meantime."

"Send my regards to them. Don't forget Aart."

"I won't."

Letters Home

Dear Rada, Kara, Leon, Arina, and Aart,

Anna and I had our first few days in Bucharest. I wanted to write for there is so much to tell you. This is a very large city. There are bigger streets, with more shops than Lipscani Street. There is this horse-drawn streetcar, or it is called a trolley. It takes people up and down a main street, picking people up and letting people off when they reach their destination. Walking does not seem to be fashionable here. We are living with Esther Prager and her daughter, Sonya. Esther owns a beautiful very large house. The house has three floors. We are living on the third floor. We have one extra-large room with two beds, a desk, two large reading chairs. There is a closet with a large white bathing tub, a white sink, and a toilet that flushes like the toilets at the train station. Esther and her daughter own this beautiful house in which paying guests are given lodging and meals. This is a place where one lives and can call home. We all have similar arrangements. We have two meals that are served each day, breakfast and dinner. All guests pay a large amount of money each week for lodgings and food. Esther has not said anything about us paying for our lodgings, but I am sure she will.

Sonya is very nice. She has taken us around and showed us where most things are in Bucharest. We are looking into a school for Anna that is not far from where we live. She can walk there. We went to a park called University Square. We ate a cold refreshment called ice cream. It was sweet and delicious. There were people selling items from tables in this park. Sonya said they are called vendors. We did not go into many stores. When I have more time, I will tell you about the people who live in the house with us. They are all very nice and helpful. Do not worry about us. We are fine! I have much more to tell you but not more time. Can you send the enclosed envelope to my family?

Affectionally, Sonia and Anna
Anna sends special hugs and kiss to Aart.

Dear Mama, Papa, Sol, and Lou,

Anna and I just returned from becoming acquainted with the city called Bucharest. It is a very large city. Anna and I had our first few days in Bucharest. I waited to write for I have much to tell you about living in this big city. There is this horse-drawn covered cart they call a streetcar. It takes people up and down a main street, picking people up and letting people off when they reach their destination. Walking does not seem to be fashionable here. Boys, you would love it. Sonya is very nice. She has taken us around and showed us where most things are in Bucharest. We are looking into a school for Anna that is not far from where we live. She can walk there. We went to a park called University Square. We ate a cold refreshment called ice cream. It was sweet and delicious. There were people selling items from tables in this park. Sonya said they are called vendors. We did not go into many stores. When I have more time, I will tell you about the people who live in the house with us. They are all very nice and helpful. We are fine. Tell Papa one of the people living here is a rabbi and his wife. He is not at all like the rabbis in Hajsyn.

We are living with Esther Prager and her daughter Sonya. Esther owns a beautiful large house. The house has three floors. We are living on the third floor. We have one extra-large room with two beds, a desk, two large reading chairs, and a room just for bathing with a large white bathing tub that has hot and cold running water, a white sink, and a toilet that flushes. Esther and her daughter own this rooming house. She rents out sections of the house to guests. We have similar arrangements. They give two meals that are served each day, breakfast and dinner. The people living here are called lodgers. They pay a large amount of money each week for the lodgings and food. Esther has not said anything about us paying for our lodgings, but I am sure she will. Papa, do not worry about money. We are fine. Do not worry about us. I have much more to tell you but not more time. We have to go downstairs for dinner. Send our thanks to Boris. He was wonderful.

Affectionally, Sonia and Anna

"ANNA, WAKE UP. YOU FELL asleep reading the paper. Did you find anything about a school?"

"No, not at all. We are going to visit the school Yankel suggested."

"Anna, come into the salon. I want to show you the best bathing tub. I decided to take a hot bath this morning. First, I had to find where the water comes from. I finally found the water levers at the top of the tub. Then I had to see what holds the water in the tub. I finally saw a round rubber plug. I inserted the plug in the hole and ran the water. The water was cold. I then found and turned the second lever that was hot. The two levers gave me hot water that was wonderful. I stepped into the tub, sat down, and enjoyed the hot water running around me. On the stool next to the tub was a bar of soap, a washcloth with a large towel. Anna, wait until you try this."

Anna said, "I will definitely try it tonight."

The gong went off, signaling dinnertime.

The conversation at dinner was about Anna's school and Sonia's classes at the university. Many evenings after dinner, the five of them would get on the streetcar and investigate parts of Bucharest. Sometimes the rabbi and his wife would join them, especially when Anna insisted they stop at the ice cream vendors.

They delayed their visit to the bank. They felt they had to learn more about the bank and the money they had on deposit. Antoine was teaching Sonia and Anna the amount of each Romanian coin and paper money. He was not aware why they wanted to know the value of the Ukraine money as well. Sonia told Antoine their father may send them Ukraine money, and they should know the value of those coins as well Romanian.

The girls had gotten acquainted with Bucharest. They knew their way to shop for food, for sundry items. They knew their way back to the house. They knew how much it cost to take the streetcar and had the money ready for the streetcar driver.

Sonia, Anna, and Yankel went to the Saint Sava School to meet with the school officials. Anna was enrolled in Saint Sava National School. Anna made friends easily. She met a few Jewish girls at school who spoke Ukrainian as well as Yiddish. She could converse with them freely. They became friends. She was loving school. Yankel would take Anna to school, and she would walk to the Jewish theatre after school.

Sonia, with Antoine's help, filled out all the requirements to enter the university. She took English and French. Sonia also enrolled in the Ciocanul (Hammer) school. This was a Jewish craft workshop. Sonia and Sura both took the course, two afternoons a week, on how to sew using the foot-pedal sewing machine. The girls wanted to make their own clothes. Sonia was busy with schools. Meeting Anna at the theatre after school was her first priority. They would all meet when possible at the theatre and walk home in the evening.

This became a routine. There were always discussions at the dinner table. Anna did not bring up the news about the war. This one particular evening after dinner, Esther asked Sonia if she could please speak to her privately. When everyone left the table, Sonia and Anna stayed behind.

Sonia said, "Esther, you wanted to speak with us?"

"Yes," said Esther. "The money your father sent me for your room and board has ran out."

Sonia looked at Anna; both were surprised that their papa sent Esther money.

"I must have what we call rent from our borders to help pay for the food and the help. I must have twenty forint each week from you and your sister."

Sonia said, "We understand. When does this start?"

"Next Friday and every Friday after that."

"You shall have it each week as requested. Thank you, Esther."

Sonia said to Anna, "Papa really looked after us. We must thank him in our next letter."

"Sonia, let's write tonight. Let's say good night to everyone."

"Anna and I have to write a letter home. Esther, thank you for the lovely dinner."

"Rabbi, Sonia and I will see you tomorrow in shul. Good night, everybody."

"Anna, we must go upstairs and count our money. We must go to the bank to meet with Mr. Solomon Bally. He is a good friend of Albert's. He is taking care of our account. Anna, do you remember the password?"

"Yes."

"What is it?"

"Kopecks."

"Yes, good. We will go tomorrow."

"No, we have to go to shul. Tomorrow is Saturday. Rabbi Morris will be upset if we are not at the services. Sonia, I will enjoy going to shul. I like getting dressed and wearing a hat. I hear the songs are beautiful."

"You are right. Forget tomorrow. We will go to shul."

"We shall go to the bank Monday afternoon after school."

"Anna, you write the letter, and I will put the ending on it. Please give me your pouch so I can empty it as well as my own."

Anna took off the pouch and gave it to Sonia. Sonia did the same. She started to separate the coins and the bills and count them.

"Anna, you have a lot of money left. How so?"

"You spend your money for the both of us each time we go anywhere."

"Well, it does not matter. It is all in one pocket. We have enough money to give Esther for three weeks and enough for us for at least five weeks."

"There is no hurry to see the banker, but we will still go on Monday."

"Anna, how are you doing with the letter? Read it to me please."

Dear Mama and Papa,

Mama, how do you feel? When do you think the baby will be born? Did you and Papa find a name for the baby? Tomorrow we are going to shul for the first time in Bucharest. The shul is of red brick and is very beautiful. It is called the choral temple. There is a very large Mogen Dovid on the front of the shul. It seems like everything is within walking distance. I will write and tell you more about the inside of the shul in my next letter.

Love to you both. Love to Lou and Sol.

Anna

Papa, Anna and I thank you for sending Esther money for our food and room. It seems that the money you sent has been spent. Now we are going to pay for food and board ourselves. Anna and I have not spent much of our coins. Rada would not let us pay for anything while we were living at her house. We did buy gifts for the family when we left. We will pay for our food and room ourselves. We still have coins. We have not touched the gold chains. We are saving as much as we can. We are keeping the chains for our trip to France. We are not sure what the ship will cost and the trains to get to France. We are going to the bank Monday to meet the banker Solomon Bally, Albert's friend. The bank is called National Bank of Bucharest. I will write you all about our meeting. Please do not worry about us. We are going to school and learning English and French so we will be able to talk in the language of the country we will be visiting. We miss everyone. Please write and let us know about the baby when it comes.

Love to Mama, Sol, and Lou.

Papa, love and kisses again. Thank you for all your help.

Sonia

"Anna, let's get ready for bed. Services start at eight thirty in the morning."

"Sonia, I am going to take my bath first."

"That is fine, Anna, but you better not stay in the tub too long."

"Sonia, I read in the paper that there is a possibility of a war coming to Bucharest."

"Anna, I just read also that war might be coming to Bucharest."

Anna said, "Yes, that is one reason I want to go to the bank on Monday."

"Anna, let's not worry about that tonight. We can pray tomorrow that it will not come here. Good night. Love you, Anna."

"Love you too, Sonia."

Going to the Temple

IT WAS JUST 7:30 A.M. when Anna was shaking Sonia to wake up.

"Sonia, I am up and dressed. Please get up."

"What is the problem?"

"I do not want to be late."

"Anna, we will be on time."

"Sonia, please brush my hair so it will shine."

"I am up now. Sit down on the bed near me, and I will brush your hair. Now will you let me get up and dressed? I will meet you downstairs."

Anna said, "See you there."

"Good morning, Anna."

"Good morning, Sura. Are you going to shul?"

"Yes. Where is Sonia?"

"She will be down shortly."

The girls were no sooner seated when Sonia came in.

"Sura, are you going to join us?"

"Yes, if you do not mind."

"Actually, I am glad. I am not sure where we are going."

"I thought so. That is why I am here this morning."

"Thank you. We appreciate that."

The girls finished their breakfast. It took them twenty minutes to walk to the shul.

Sura said, "We have to go upstairs. Women upstairs, and men downstairs."

Anna said, "Yes, we are aware."

The girls got seated next to Faygie. The rabbi walked to the bimah. He started to chant. The music started, and the choir began singing. Anna and Sonia were so moved by the music they started to cry. The girls sat mesmerized throughout the entire service. When the service was over, Faygie asked the girls how they were feeling.

Anna said, "I never heard or saw anything so beautiful."

Sonia was still in amazement at the service. She finally asked, "Is this done every day?"

Faygie answered, "No, only on the Sabbath. The high holidays are even more beautiful. Just wait. Come, we have to go downstairs and meet Morris. They have breakfast after Saturday's service. The ladies make the food and bring it in for breakfast."

We walked down the stairs and were met with a group of well-dressed people all wishing each other "*Geten Shabbas.*" Rabbi Morris came and kissed Faygie and greeted us.

Anna and Sonia said at the same time, "What a beautiful service!"

"Thank you. Come, let's eat before there will be nothing left."

The girls were surprised to see such an overabundance of food on one table. People were walking around the table with plates in their hand, taking food off the table and putting it in their plates.

Anna said, "We ate before we came."

Sonia said, "We are going to leave, Faygie. You and the rabbi have many people to meet. This was a beautiful experience. Thank you for asking us to come. Tell Rabbi we will see him at home. *Shabbet shalom.*"

As we walked to the door, Sura asked, "What kind of service do you have in Hajsyn on the Sabbath?"

"We have never been to a service."

"Women only go on high holiday services."

"Oh, this must have been quite a show for you."

"Yes," said Anna. "It was beautiful. The inside of the shul looked interesting. We will have to go back when there are no people so we can really see the inside."

Sura asked, "Anna, where did you get that hat?"

"Sonia and I went shopping for hats last week. We knew we had to wear a hat in shul, and we did not have one. What would you like to do today?"

Learning Bucharest

March 15, 1919

"LET'S TAKE A RIDE ON the streetcar and see where we would like to get off."

"That is fine with me," said Sura.

Sonia was still thinking about the beautiful music. She finally said, "Yes, let's go."

The girls got on the streetcar. Sura decided they should get off at Herastrau Park. There were many things to see and do. There was a boat rental complex and fairgrounds with a carousel.

Anna asked, "What is a carousel?"

"Just you wait and see."

The streetcar driver announced, "Baneasa Bridge."

Sura said, "This is where we get off. We will walk over to the bridge. That is where all the exciting things are."

Anna wanted to know what things were in that park.

Sura said, "First, there is a big carousel that you can ride on a wooden horse. The horse can also go up and down. There are boat rides that go under the bridge. They are called ferries. There are eating places and, of course, ice cream stalls."

The girls could not believe there were so many things that one person could see and do in this lovely large park. The first thing to do was ride the carousel. It was free. When it stopped going around, they hopped on and found a horse they would like to sit on.

Sura said, "I will help you get on the first time. After that, you will definitely do it yourself. Hurry, the carousel is stopping. Ann, do you need help?"

"No, I can manage."

"How about you, Sonia?"

"No, I am fine. I will just grab this tall metal bar. Anna, grab that bar and pull yourself up on to the carousel."

"Anna, what color horse do you like?"

Anna said, "Pink."

"Fine. I will put you on that horse. Now hold on to that pole and put the strap around you. Hold on tight for the horse will start to go up and down when the music starts. Sonia, how are you doing?"

"I am on a horse and holding on."

"I will be sitting next to Anna in case she needs help."

"Thank you, Sura."

The music started, and the carousel started to go around.

"Remember, hold on tight. The horse will start to go up and down."

As soon as Sura said that, up went Anna's horse. Sonia's horse also went up. Then Sura's followed. The girls started to laugh.

"This is wonderful," said Anna. As the carousel stopped, Anna asked, "Can we stay on this for another ride?"

"Yes, but only one more time. You can get dizzy from too many rides at one time."

The girls stayed for one more time around. It was a little difficult getting off the horse. Sonia was a bit dizzy. She had to sit for a few minutes. She was not a fan of the carousel. When Sonia was feeling better, the girls started around the park. Sonia noticed a large building across the street.

She asked Sura, "What is in that building?"

Sura answered, "That is the national bank building."

"Oh," responded Anna.

Before Anna could say another word, Sonia said, "That is a large interesting building. Can we walk to the lake?"

Sura said, "We can take a boat trip around the lake."

Sonia said, "Not today please."

Sura said, "Come, I will take you to some beautiful houses where the very rich live."

Anna said, "Your house is beautiful."

"Yes, but these have stained-glass windows and skylights. These homes are just in the next street."

They decided to walk down Soseaua Kiseleff. Sura was definitely right. Each house was more beautiful than the other. They walked around the area and ended back where they started.

It was getting late. Anna said, "Let's get on the next streetcar home."

All agreed. The streetcar stopped in front of them, and they boarded.

Sura said, "Anna you tell us where to get off."

"That is a good idea. Anna, it is up to you where we get off."

The girls found seats and chatted a bit when Anna finally said, "The next stop please."

Sura said, "That is right. We will not worry for you do know your way home."

The girls got off the streetcar. They walked home.

Anna said to Sonia, "I am waiting for the newspaper. I will be in as soon as the paper arrives."

Sonia went upstairs. She was still not feeling herself. She wanted to take a hot bath. There was plenty of time till dinner.

Anna sat in one of the rocking chairs, waiting for the paper. The young boy delivering the paper handed it to Anna, then said, "Have a good day." He went on his way. Anna was disappointed. The handsome tall boy did not pass by today. She was hoping to see him again.

As Anna entered their room, Sonia called out, "Anna is that you?"

Anna answered, "Yes."

"I will be out of the bath soon."

"That is all right. I will take my bath tonight."

"All right." Hearing that, Sonia lay back in the tub and enjoyed her bath.

Anna sat down to read the paper while Sonia was in the tub.

Sonia said, "Anna, please be careful about the bank. Nobody is to know we have money there."

"Yes, I forgot. I'm sorry."

"We will go there on Monday. We will introduce ourselves to Mr. Solomon Bally. We will ask him to deposit money to our account in the bank in Marseille. I will have to find out the name of that bank. Albert had set up an account in our names. I want to put most of the money in the Marseille bank. We have to make sure we have enough money for our tickets. Papa gave me all the instructions in his letter, the accounts and numbers.

"Let's get dressed for the gong will soon ring. Sura said the boys and she planned fun day. We are all going to the fairgrounds tomorrow. We should wear comfortable shoes. We will be doing a lot of walking."

As the girls approached their door, the dinner gong went off. It seemed all of them came to the dining room together. Rabbi and his wife were at the temple. Services began 8:30 a.m. and at 7:00 p.m. on Fridays and Saturdays. All rabbis were required to be in shul on the weekends. During the week and Sundays, they had a schedule.

The girls sat down, said the prayers, and ate their dinner.

Sonia said, "We went to services. The temple was beautiful. The music made me cry. We said the prayers. The food display was plentiful. Everything was beautiful. We did not stay for the food. Papa would love this shul. That reminds me—Anna, did you start the letter to Mama and Papa?"

"Yes, it is on the desk. I will finish it when we go upstairs."

Yankel asked, "What did you do after services?"

Anna was the first to answer. "We went on a carousel."

Sura answered, "We went to the fairgrounds. We rode the carousel twice. Sonia got dizzy. We then went to Soseaua Kisileff. We saw some beautiful homes. We came home. Sonia was not feeling good."

Anna said, "We must get walking shoes."

Sonia said, "I want to be able to go tomorrow. I am going to bed."

Anna said, "I will go with you."

The girls thanked Esther for a lovely dinner, then said good night.

Sonia asked, "Is the letter on the desk?"

"Yes."

"I will finish it tomorrow. I am not feeling good. I must lie down. Anna, why don't you take your bath."

"That sounds good to me. Sonia, good night. Feel better."

After her bath, Anna finished the letter so it can get posted tomorrow.

The Baby Is Born

LIFE IN HAJSYN PASSED QUIETLY. Boris would come every other Saturday. He and Avraham would go into the barn to smoke a cigar and read the girls' letters. The family enjoyed the letters. They could not believe the things the girls were writing. What fascinated everyone was the ice cream, the bathtub, and the toilet.

The boys were packing groceries. Each were getting kopecks and saving them. Raisa helped Avraham in the store until it was evident she was too pregnant. Everyone was happy for the Zitefsky family. Everyone felt Raisa was not herself since the accident. Time was passing slowly for Raisa. Her letters told about her lovely new kitchen and what she was knitting for the new baby. Avraham was happy that the girls were safe. Everyone was pleased that the letters were flowing back and forth.

The baby clothes she was sewing were pink. Raisa definitely wanted a girl. All the material she bought for the baby were pink. She looked forward to Boris's visits. He would bring letters from the girls. Raisa felt badly. After the letters were read, they had to be burned. She would have wanted to read them again and again.

This particular Saturday, Boris came to the store. Avraham and Boris went off to the barn to smoke their cigars. They discussed the news of the times. Boris gave Avraham the two letters he received from Rada.

Avraham said to Boris, "I have never asked you. Do the girls write to you?"

"Yes, Sonia and Anna both write to me. They write pretty much the same things. I do enjoy their letters. Sonia writes to Rada as well."

"I am happy to know that."

100

Sol came running into the barn. "Something is wrong with Mommy."

"Sol, hurry up. Run down to Mrs. Klein's house. Tell her Mommy is having the baby. She must come immediately. Sol, just bring her back with you. Boris, would you go up to the house and see to Raisa so I can close the store?"

Boris ran in one direction, while Avraham ran to close the store. Lou was trying to help in the store as best he could.

Avraham entered the store and announced, "I am sorry. I have to close the store. Raisa is having the baby now."

Everyone understood. They started to congratulate him. He and Lou started to push people out of the door. It took them all of fifteen minutes to close the store.

Rushing back to the house, Avraham said to Lou, "Mommy is going to be all right. We are going to have a new baby in the house. Do not worry." When they entered the house, Avraham asked Raisa, "How are you feeling?"

She answered, "Not very good. It feels like it is going to be very soon. Where is Mrs. Klien?"

"Sol went to get her."

Boris said his goodbye. The both of them said, "Thank you for helping."

Boris said, "Have a healthy baby." He then went out the kitchen door.

Sol came rushing in the front door carrying Mrs. Klien's black bag. Mrs. Klien was following behind him. She immediately took over. She told Sol and Lou to leave the room. She asked Avraham to get the package she left earlier for this particular day. Avraham brought in the package. Mrs. Klien asked Avraham to leave.

"We will be fine."

Avraham told the boys to come with him. They had to close the store properly.

Raisa had the girl she wanted. Avraham kept his promise. They named the little girl Reba after Raisa's mother. Everyone doted on Reba. She was beautiful and had big brown eyes. Avraham said she was the most beautiful child. Avraham felt he had lost his two girls when they went away. Reba had taken their place. He was truly smitten.

Raisa wrote a short letter to the girls, telling them that the baby was born. They named her Reba. She was as beautiful as they were. Raisa promised to write more later. Avraham also wrote,

> Girls, Mama is fine, and Reba is eating and doing well. The boys are excited about the baby. They do have many questions. They want to know why won't she talk and walk, when will she be able to play with them. We explained this does not happen till she is one or two years old. Boris has been to see her. He said she is tiny and won't pick her up. We will write more later.
>
> Love, Papa and Mama

Avraham insisted on putting Reba to bed each night. Raisa was enjoying dressing her and showing her off in the store. Many of the customers brought gifts for the baby. They saw a big change in Raisa.

Meanwhile, this morning at breakfast in Bucharest, Sura announced, "There is a letter for the both of you. It came yesterday, but my mother forgot to give it to you. She knew you were not feeling well. She was concerned it maybe bad news."

Sonia opened the letter, read it, and handed it to Anna.

Anna read it and said, "We have a big announcement. Our mother had a baby girl. They named her Reba."

Sonia said, "Now we have some shopping to do."

Breakfast was finished. The three girls and the two young men started off on their fun day.

The group took the streetcar and got off at Herastrau Park. There were many things to see and do there. There was a boat rental complex, a swimming area. There was a large eating area, and it had a shopping area.

"It is also not too far from the fairgrounds where you, Sonia, can ride the carousel."

"Are you teasing me, Yankel?"

"Yes, I am. If I may ask, how are you feeling?"

"I am fine, thank you. But I will stay off the carousel today."

Everyone laughed.

"I wonder if there are any baby stores in the shopping area. Anna and I do want to send something home for the baby."

The first stop was walking around Herastrau Park.

Anna said to Sonia, "My feet are going to hurt today."

"Maybe there is a shoe store in the park. Can we walk toward the shopping area? Anna needs shoes."

"We will do that first."

"Good, I will get shoes as well."

They walked past the lake where the boats were docked. They passed a few eating restaurants near the lake. They were beginning to see buildings on either side of a strip of grass.

Antoine said, "There is the shopping area."

They walked down the strip, seeing many interesting shops but not the two they needed. As they got to the end of the strip, they spotted a shoe store. Anna was delighted. They all piled into the shop.

Anna said, "I need a pair of walking shoes."

The salesperson asked, "What shoe size are you.?"

Anna replied, "I do not know."

"That's all right. We can measure your foot for you."

Anna said, "Thank you." Anna was wondering, *How will he do that?*

The salesperson said, "Please take your shoes off." He then put a metal ruler on the floor and asked Anna to put her foot on the ruler.

"You are a size 6."

Sonia said, "I too need walking shoes."

"Take your shoe off, and I will measure your foot as well. You need a size 5 shoe. You have tiny feet." The salesperson said, "I will be back with some shoes for both of you."

The girls tried on a few pairs, and everyone had an opinion. Finally, each girl found a comfortable pair of walking shoes. They wore the new pair and put their old shoes in the shopping bag. They looked for a baby or children's shop. There were none. They walked completely around the lake.

Sura said, "Let's have lunch."

The boys said, "We thought you would never ask."

There was a delightful outdoor restaurant that looked like a large coffee cup. You walked into the cup to be seated. They decided to eat there. They were handed a menu and were given utensils inside a napkin held together by a round band that looked like a coffee cup.

Sura said, "I have never been here before. This is very fancy."

Sonia said, "We will all pay for lunch ourselves. The boys paid for ice cream the last time."

That started the conversation. They talked about everything. When the subject of the war was approached, Antoine said, "Lets finish our lunch and enjoy the day."

Lunch came and was eaten. The group was off to the fairgrounds. They spent the remainder of the day trying the amusements. All but Sonia went on the carousel.

They walked toward the streetcar and took the next one going home. It was getting dark, and Esther did not like her borders being late for dinner.

Anna said, "We did not get ice cream."

Sura responded, "We will have that for dessert."

"Oh," said Anna.

There was enough time for everyone to wash before the gong would sound.

Anna said, "I will be up shortly. I am waiting for the paper." Anna sat in one of the rocking chairs, waiting for the paper. When that handsome young man came walking down the street, he again smiled at Anna. She smiled back. He went on his way. The paper came shortly after. She took it and went up to her room to wash for dinner.

Anna decided to read some of the newspaper. There was time before dinner. The newspaper headline read, "Is War Coming to Bucharest." The paper went on to write that the kingdom of Romania has declared neutrality and will not participate in the war. The article went on to say that Romania's natural resources of petroleum and their ability to export food will keep them out of the war. Anna woke Sonia up. She was upset.

"Sonia, the newspaper said there may be a war in Romania."

"Anna, that is not a nice way to wake someone up."

"Really, see for yourself."

Sonia started to read the paper.

Anna said, "The paper said there may not be a war. Let's go down and ask the boys. They will know more than we do."

"Let me get dressed, then we will go down. The gong will be ringing soon. Anna, why are you not changing?"

"I am upset. Do you think Papa will be going to war?"

"No, he is too old."

"How about Boris?"

"Yes, he is a soldier. Let's write to Rada."

"I hope Boris will be safe."

The girls started down the stairs. They met the rabbi and Faygie. They too were discussing the article in the paper. When they met the girls, they stopped talking.

Sonia said, "It is all right. We read the article in the paper too."

They entered the dining room. The boys were standing and talking. When they saw the girls, they helped them into their seats. They all started to talk about the coming war. Everyone's question is, will the men be taken into the army? There was nothing in the paper about a draft or any army being formed.

Antoine spoke first. "I am not a citizen of Romania. I may have to go back to France."

Yankel said, "I am a citizen of Romania. I may be drafted. We will have to see how this plays out. Let's have dinner."

Anna asked, "Does anyone know what is happening in Ukraine? Are they in the war?"

"Nobody knows. Ukraine has not announced. It seems Great Britain, France, Italy, Japan, the United States, and Russia are forming an alliance against Germany. Nobody is moving fast or marching into any land yet."

Rabbi Morris said, "I will have to enlist in some armed forces. I am not sure what service a clergyman will be assigned to. Let's not ruin this fine dinner that Esther made."

Faygie said, "Well, Sonia, did you ride the carousel today?"

"No, thank you. Anna and I each bought a pair of walking shoes. There are lots of fun things at the fairgrounds. There was an unusual eating place that was shaped like a coffee cup. You actually went into the cup to be seated. That was interesting and fun."

"I have never eaten in a coffee cup before," said Anna.

The conversation went from the war back to more pleasant things. The ladies came to take their order for dessert. Anna did not wait for them to ask.

She said, "Chocolate ice cream please and some cookies."

Everyone started to laugh.

Rabbi Morris said, "Anna, are you sure you want ice cream?"

"Oh, yes. I did not get any while we were near the vendors."

The remainder of the borders ordered their dessert.

Sonia said, "I will have the same as Anna."

Rabbi Morris and Faygie went for their usual walk, while the team of five went to play a game of cards.

Yankel said, the rabbi will have to go to the army if Romania gets into the war."

Sonia asked, "Yankel, how about you?"

"I had a broken kneecap that never healed correctly. I will not be able to march. Let's hope war will never come to Bucharest."

The card game continued for another hour.

Sonia said, "I am sorry to break up the card game early. I would like to write a letter home. I am concerned that if Ukraine gets involved in the war, our father will have to go."

Anna said, "I will say good night as well."

Both girls started up the stairs.

Sonia closed their bedroom door. She said, "We do have to get to the bank. We must transfer some of that money before the banks will not be able to exchange money from country to country."

"Sonia, how do you know that?"

"Papa told me what we must do if this should happen. We must go to the bank. The money we have here and the gold necklaces will stay with us. We have to see how much is in the bank and how much we need for the ship's fare to America. I hope Mr. Solomon Bally will have answers for us. Anna, I am going to write a letter to Papa. Take a hot bath, then go to bed."

"Sonia, I am going to read the comics, write a letter to Mama. I want to know what Reba is doing. I will then go to bed."

It took six months before a letter came from Rada. She wrote that there was a war on but no fighting in her country. It seemed the fighting was in Germany, Austria, Hungary, Bulgaria, and the Ottoman Empire.

Rada wrote,

> I am passing a letter from the Zitefsky family. I hope all is well. Is there fighting in Bucharest? How are you both doing? Do write. It takes a long time for the mail to get someplace. I will write more later. I knew you wanted this letter.
>
> I send the love of the children, Leon, and me.

Sura got the mail from the postman this particular morning. Sonia and Anna had just come for breakfast when Sura stopped them. Sura said, "You got a letter from home."

"Thank you, Sura."

Esther has not rung the gong. This gave the girls time to open and read the letter.

It was a long letter. Anna said, "Read it to me."

"I think this should be read in our room."

"All right, let's have breakfast, then we will read it in our room. Sonia, is anybody hurt?"

"No."

"Has anybody died?"

"No, but this is a very private letter to both of us. It is not for anyone else to read. Let's rush through breakfast."

The gong just rang, and both girls rushed in, ate a rather small meal, then excused themselves.

"Sonia, you frightened me. Is something wrong?"

"Papa got shot. But I could not finish the letter. Let's go up to our room and read it."

"We are here. Read the letter, please."

"Papa wrote it."

Avraham wrote,

> This particular day, Boris came in very excited and very much upset. He and I went into the barn. He told me we are at war. It was just announced. All able-bodied men are being drafted into the army. Age does not matter. Boris said, "I have bad news for you. The commandant has orders for you on his desk. You are to be deployed in four weeks. You must go!" I told him, "How can I go. I have responsibilities to the people in the community." He said, "Do you think the army really cares? They are calling men of all ages. You will have to join the army."
>
> I got very quiet for a moment, then I started to laugh. I told him, "Then you might as well shoot me in the leg. They would not take a person with a leg wound." To my surprise, the next few minutes were unbelievable. Boris took his gun out of the holster and shot me in the left leg. The shot was heard in the store. Raisa, the boys, and a few of the customers in the store came running into the barn. Boris said, "We were testing a gun when Mr. Zitefsky took the gun. He dropped it. The gun hit the floor. It went off and hit him in the leg."
>
> Boris had Sol and Lou running for towels and wood strips. He needed them to stop the bleeding and brace the leg. Raisa and Boris

inspected the wound. Boris told me it was a bad shot. The bullet hit the leg bone. Lou and Sol came back with the supplies Boris needed. Boris tied the towel strips around my leg to stop the bleeding. Sol and Lou held the wood tight around my leg, while Boris tied towel strips to support the wounded leg.

Before everyone left the barn, I said, "Mr. Constable, could you help me into the house?" Boris replied, "Mr. Zitefsky, I am sorry this happened. I came only to inform you that we are at war and for you to inform your community." Boris and I made it clear that he was there to do his duty, to inform me and the community of the war.

Raisa and the boys went back to the store. They told the customers that the constable was testing a gun. It fell to the floor and went off and hit me in the leg bone.

The bullet did not hit the bone. We just had to stop the bleeding. I will be fine in a week. I must wear a bandage and the wood brace for six to eight weeks. The army will have taken all the men from this area. The army will have forgotten me.

The commandant has made Boris the second-in-command. He will not be on the front line. You are not to send him any letters. Boris sends his love and hope you are safe in Bucharest. When Boris write to Rada, she will forward his letters. Girls, I am fine. My leg is healing. I am able to walk on it. We are concerned about you. Is there fighting in Bucharest? Please write to Rada. We are concerned. There is no fighting in Ukraine. So far, we are safe. When this war is over, we will all go to America. God be with you.

Love, Mama, Sol, Lou, and Reba

I forgot to tell you. Reba is walking. She wants to be with the boys. Each held her hand, and she was walking. Then one morning, the boys forgot her. The next thing we knew, she got up from the floor and just started to walk.

Rada got her letter from Boris. Included in the envelope were the letters from the Zitefsky family and a short note from Boris for the girls.

Dear Sonia and Anna,

I have to go to fight against the Germans. I will not be in the front lines. Please do not write to me. Someone may see me reading one of your wonderful letters. I will send you notes through Rada. I miss the both of you.

Fondly, Boris

The girls finished reading their letters. They could not believe what their papa was writing. They definitely could not read this downstairs.

"Papa is fine, and thank God he did not go to war."

"Thanks to Boris."

"I have to get the letter with the information Papa gave me to give to the banker. Anna, do you remember the password?"

"Yes, kopecks."

"Good."

"Why do you keep asking me?"

"The banker will ask you your password. This was just in case something happened to me. You will still be able to get to America."

"Oh," remarked Anna. "Papa really thought of everything."

"When we go downstairs, Anna, we will tell them that Reba is walking and needs shoes. They do not have any in her size. She is walking in socks, and she keeps falling. Mama asked us to see if we can find something for her in one of those lovely shops we keep writing about."

"Sonia, you are so smart."

"Anna, do you have carfare for the streetcar?"

"I do not have any classes today at the university. I will meet you in the Jewish theatre after school."

"Let's go downstairs. Yankel is waiting for you. Sura and I are going to take a lesson on the sewing machine."

As the girls approached the bottom step, Yankel was waiting for Anna. "Anna, let's go. We don't want to be late for school."

Anna and Yankel rushed off to get Anna to school on time. Sonia and Sura started to leave for the Jewish craft workshop to continue learning how to use the foot-pedal sewing machine. Esther came out on the porch and handed each of them a bag. She said it was a small lunch. They thanked her and went on their way. The school was not far from the Jewish theatre. They walked there.

Sura asked, "Was there bad news in the letter?"

"Yes, my father got shot in the leg."

"Is he okay? Yes, we did not get that far in the letter when we saw the word *shot*. We decided it was private. We should read the letter upstairs. My little sister is going to be spoiled. The boys are with her when they have any free time." The remainder of the conversation revolved around Reba.

The morning went quickly. Sura and Sonia stopped at a park bench to eat their lunch. They decided to walk around the area. They passed a sweet shop and purchased a bag full of cookies. They arrived just as Anna and her friends were approaching the theatre.

Sonia said, "Anyone for cookies? Anna, are you ready to go shopping? We may have time to stop at a hat shop."

Anna and Sonia said goodbye. They went on their way. They walked to the car stop and waited for the next car to come.

"Sonia, do you know where we are going?"

"I know where we have to get off the streetcar. We know it is the tallest building in the area."

Anna said, "Thank you for the cookies. They were delicious."

"I thought you might be hungry. I think the next stop is ours."

"Yes, it is. Let's get off as soon as the streetcar stops."

Both girls looked around for the tall building.

Anna said, "There it is on your right."

"Yes, you are correct. Let's cross the street."

"You know, it is near the street where all the wealthy people live."

"Well, one day we will have houses like that. Anna, let's get to America all right."

They approached this beautiful building. It had extremely large columns in the entrance and very large glass doors that looked like they would be difficult to open. There were men dressed in blue-and-red uniforms assigned to open the doors. As they entered the bank, there was an enormous central banking hall with a marble floor and columns inside.

Anna asked me, "What do we do now?"

"Let's ask one of the men in uniform where we can find Mr. Solomon Bally. Excuse me, sir. We are looking for Mr. Solomon Bally. Could you direct us to his office?"

"You both are looking for Mr. Bally?"

"Yes, we have business with him."

"Really. Well, tell me what you need him for, and I will get him."

Sonia said, "We have business to discuss with him."

"I am sorry, girls. He is a busy man. I cannot disturb him."

"He has our money in this bank."

"Well, maybe you should come back another day."

Behind the girls, they heard a woman's voice very quietly saying, "These young ladies said they have business with Mr. Solomon Bally. Now would you please take them to his office."

Sonia turned around and said, "Dora!" She put her arms around her. "How wonderful to see you and at this time."

Dora again said, "These young ladies have business with Mr. Bally."

The man in the red coat said, "Follow me."

Dora took us by the hand and said, "Come with me."

We walked across the marble floor to a section of the bank that had two desks with men dressed in business suits busy writing. Behind them was this heavyset gentleman.

He looked up, got up from his chair, and said, "Dora, did you forget something?"

"No, Solomon. I brought you two new customers. Well, let me introduce Sonia and Anna Zitefsky. They said they have business with you."

"We are friends of Albert Lebad, from the bank in Podil."

"Oh, yes, I have been waiting for you. I thought you would have been here sooner. I guess you still have funds."

"Yes," said Sonia. "With the war coming, my sister and I thought that we should come to meet you. We were thinking of moving some money that our father sent to your bank to the bank in Marseille. When we arrive in France, we are going to need money for the ship fare and the trains to get to France. We felt some of the money should be in the Marseille bank."

"Albert Lebad and I are good friends. I heard about your quest to America. I will do all I can to get you to Marseille. I will transfer whatever you need. Just come into the bank and show them this card. You will have no further problems to see me. Now what is it that we are doing today?"

Dora said, "Should I leave?"

"No, please stay," Sonia said. "I am going to need your help, if you do not mind."

"I will help you."

Sonia now turned to Mr. Bally. "Mr. Albert Lebad from the merchants trading exchange had set up a fund for my sister and I. We are going to need money for room and board for one more year. We will need train fare to get to Marseille, France. We will need money for the ship to get us to America. We have to get to Philadelphia. The French line called Fabre Line. We do not know the name of the ship, only the line. It is called Fabre Line. It is the only ship that goes directly into Philadelphia and Providence. Our aunt wrote and told us this Fabre ship line is the only line for Philadelphia."

"You do know there is a war going on. All passenger ships and immigrant ships are being used for soldiers. You will not be able to travel till the war is over. So I suggest that you leave the money in this bank. I have no control over the French banks. I will set up an account for you and your sister. You will be able to come into the bank and get money whenever you need it. I will put a limit on your withdrawals. If you need more funds than you are allowed, you can then come and see me. Being you are minors, this will stop anyone from using your accounts. Is that all right with you, Dora?"

"Sonia is doing a good job. Deal with her please."

Sonia asked, "Anna, is that all right with you?"

"Again I am saying I will give each of you a bank card with your name and a special number on the card. When you want money, just come into the bank and present this card. The bank teller will do the rest. My signature must go on slip when a withdrawal will be made. That is the stipulation Albert made when we last spoke. Do you need any money now?"

"We have enough for three or four weeks meals and five weeks spending money."

"Good. Are we finished with your transactions today? Thank you, ladies, for coming in today. Dora, I forgot something in your transaction. Could you please stay a minute? I was just about to have one of the guards call you back to my office, of course."

"Girls, do you have time to wait for me? I am sure this will not take long."

Mr. Bally came from around his desk and shook the girls' hands. He said, "It was very nice meeting you. I know I will be seeing you again. I will try to find out more information about the ship you want to sail to America. We will find the easiest way to travel to Marseille. We have time to discuss your trip after the war."

After the girls left, Mr. Bally wanted to know how Dora met the girls.

"I have to tell you there is quite a story about them. The parents had to send them away. There were these small wars called pogroms in many of the Ukrainian villages where Jews live. About two years ago, in their village, there was one of these pogroms. They were killing small girls between the ages of seven to fourteen. Their father hid them in the outhouse for two days to protect them. They were not touched. They only had water to drink. Their mother has a sister in America. That is where they are headed. Their father has a friend that took the girls over a frozen river in the dead of winter. They had no papers. If caught, they would have been killed. Whoever this friend was is truly a friend. They were hidden until they got papers to go into Bucharest. They are going to need papers to get into France. Let's talk about that later."

"I just wanted to know their story. I may need your help."

"When we meet again, I will tell you how I met them."

"Thank you for the information. I think I can help them."

"Goodbye, Solomon."

"See you soon, Dora."

The girls waited for Dora to come out of the bank. Sonia asked, "Is everything all right with your account?"

"Yes, I just forgot to sign a few papers."

Anna said, "We are going to the streetcar. Is that how you are going home?"

"No, Anna. I live just in the very next street. Next Sunday, please come for dinner. Here is my card, just in case you lost the first card."

Sonia said, "Thank you. We would love to come. Goodbye, Dora. We will see you Sunday."

"Dora, would you know of a toy store or a baby shop? My parents wrote that we have a new baby sister, and we want to send her something."

Dora thought to herself, *How are they going to do that? Best to keep my mouth shut till I find out the entire story.* "Yes, there is a small apothecary shop down this street that may carry some toys or baby booties."

"Thank you, Dora."

With that, the girls went down the street that Dora pointed out. Sonia asked Anna, "What do you think about the banker?"

"He is very polite. He seems to know Albert Lebad. I did not want to ask how much money is in our account for Dora was with us. We will just have to trust this bank in Bucharest and Mr. Bally."

Anna and Sonia walked down the street Dora pointed out. There were a few lovely shops—a bakery, a shoe store, a hat store, and the apothecary.

"Let's visit the hat shop, Sonia."

"Only if we have time. We must be home for dinner, or everyone will worry."

Their first stop was the apothecary shop. The store smelled of medicines. There was a man dressed with a white jacket and a name embroidered on the front of the jacket. Sonia asked him if they had any toys or clothes for babies or little girls.

The man smiled and answered, "Yes, we do. Did your mother have a baby?"

"Yes. Could you show us where the shoes are?"

"Go straight back to the wall. Make a left, and you will see a counter full of toys and some booties."

"Thank you." Turning to Anna, Sonia said, "The booties are the important item. Let's try and get them in different sizes."

Anna found a pair of pink booties and a larger pair of white ones. "Let's take both."

"Is there a small soft doll on the counter?"

"No, but there is one inside the glass cabinet."

"Sir," Sonia called to the man in the white coat. "Is it possible that we could buy that cute soft doll?"

"Yes, you can. Is there anything else I can help you with?"

Sonia answered, "No, thank you. We have all we need. How much do we owe you?"

"The booties are one forint each, and the doll is three forints."

"That is expensive for a doll."

"Yes, I know. I do not set the price."

"We will take both the booties and the doll. Can you wrap them as a gift?"

"Sorry, I only have a pink bag to put them in."

"That will be fine."

The girls left the store.

Sonia said, "We will not have time to visit the hat shop. We will make sure we come back. Let's catch the next streetcar home."

The girls just made it home as the gong was ringing.

Sura said, "Just in time."

"Wait till you see what we got for Reba. We will show it to you after dinner."

Dinner and dessert were served. There was much discussion during dinner about Romania being neutral.

Sonia asked, "What does being neutral mean?"

Antoine said, "The country of Romania is not going to fight in this war. Both sides that are fighting agreed to that. At least for now. Romania has a large supply of petroleum that both sides need for their tanks."

After dinner, the discussion turned to baby booties. Sonia brought the pink bag to the table. She took out the booties.

Faygie said, "They are beautiful. May I see them?"

Anna handed them to Faygie. She said, "They are two sizes. We were not sure of the size of her feet." Anna brought out the doll. The tag said "Raggedy Ann." This doll had red yarn for hair and a triangle nose. "We thought Reba would like the red hair on this doll.

The next few months, all was quiet in Bucharest. They were beginning to see soldiers with all different uniforms speaking different languages. Anna was frightened by the army uniforms. She would not go outside alone. She would not even go outside and wait for the newspaper. Yankel would take her to school, and he would have to go pick her up after school. Sura would meet Sonia at the Ciocanul (Hammer) school after classes were over at the university. Sonia and Sura were both learning to use the foot-pedal sewing machine. Sonia made a blue skirt, and Sura made a velvet vest. Once you made a project, and it fitted, you graduated from the course.

Sonia and Anna decided to make some money by working. Anna was feeling a bit more secure. She would again sit outside waiting for the paper and hoping to see the tall young boy pass by. He never did come by again.

Anna got the paper and saw an advertisement for a governess/babysitter. There were a few positions opened. Only one seemed interesting. The children were six and four years old. Both were girls. They only lived two blocks away. The hours were from three till six, two days weekdays and all day Saturday from 10:00 a.m. till 6:00 p.m.

"Anna, are you sure you would not like to work in a candy store or the bakery?"

"No, I enjoy playing with children."

"What day and time do you want to go?"

"I get out of school at 2:30 p.m. If you can meet me at school, we can then see how long it takes to walk to their house."

"Anna, I will not be able to take you during the week. Some days I do not get out of school till 3:30 p.m."

"We will talk to Yankel and see what his schedule is like."

The gong rang, and Anna rushed upstairs to brush her hair and wash her face. As Anna was going up, Sonia was going down the stairs.

Sonia said, "Make it fast so we can talk to Yankel.'

They all were seated and dinner was served.

Yankel said, "I must excuse myself after dinner. I have to go back to the theatre. The prompter got angry at the main star and left. I must go back to the theatre, go through the script so I know where the actors are at in case they forget their lines. My Yiddish is not fast. I hope they all know their lines."

Sonia asked, "What is a prompter?"

"That is the person that follows the play from beginning to end. If an actor forgets their lines, they tell the actors what they are to say. The show must go on. No one should forget their lines."

Sonia said, "Do you have the book with you?"

"Yes," said Yankel.

"May I see it?"

"Sure. How is your Yiddish?"

"Good."

"Can you read these lines on page 4? It is a song the grandmother is teaching her grandchildren."

"Well, let's see." Sonia started to sing the song.

The song Sonia sang in Yiddish
(English translation)

OYFN PRIPETSHIK BRENT A FAYERLIN (The fireplace burns a fire)

UN DER SHTUB IZ HEYSAND (The room is hot)

UN DER REBE LERNTAND (The rabbi teaches)

KLEYN KINDERLEKHLITTLE (children)

DEM ALEF-BETZTHE (*A*s and the *B*s)

UN DER REBE LERNTAND (The rabbi teaches)

KLEYN KINDERLEKHLITTLE (children)

DEM ALEF-BETZTHE (*A*s and *B*s)

A big smile broke out on Yankel's face. "Sonia, will you come with me this evening? There is a performance. It starts at 8:30 p.m. I really need you."

"I will not be in front of people?"

"No, not at all."

"Yes, I will be happy to go with you."

Anna said, "Sonia, you don't mind if I stay home? I want to take a hot bath."

"Not at all. We will see you later."

"Sonia, we have to leave now."

"I am coming, Yankel."

They went out the front door and flew down the stairs.

Yankel said, "You saved my life tonight. Thank you!"

"After all you have done for Anna and me, this is the least I could do for you."

That night, the show went on without a problem. The performers were happy. The audience enjoyed the show. Sonia enjoyed being in the theatre. Yankel was overjoyed because everything went off without a problem.

"Sonia, I will be with you. I have to count the money we took in this evening. I will just put the cash in the vault and count it tomorrow." On the way home, Yankel remarked, "Your Yiddish is excellent."

"That is all we spoke at home."

"Let me ask you. Would you like the job being the prompter until you leave for America?"

"How often will I have to work?"

"You would have to be at the theater every evening we have a show. There is a Sunday evening performance. We are closed Mondays, Fridays, and Saturday all day and night. You have to read the script and know it well. It is always in Yiddish. When we are practicing for a new show, you will not have to be here. When the actors learn their lines, then you will work with them."

"How much are you paying for this service?"

"When you will be working, you will get twenty-five forint a week. When you are not working, you will get fifteen forint a week. You may have to come in from time to time on the weeks you are considered not working. The actors may need your help with their lines. When we are having shows, you will be working all week."

"That is a beautiful offer. I have to talk it over with Anna. I know she will not object. Can I let you know tomorrow?"

"Yes! Sonia, do you want to stop for tea and a cake."

"That would be nice."

"There is a coffee shop around the corner that is still open."

They walked to the coffee shop and found it open. When they entered the shop, the owner greeted Yankel. He seated them immediately. The waiter came. He asked if they were ready to order.

Sonia said, "Yes. I will have a cup of coffee and a slice of apple pie."

Yankel smiled. He said, "That is the first. No tea? No muffin?"

"I have to try other things to eat sometimes. If I am going to be eating with the cast, I should try other foods and desserts."

"Sonia, you would fit in anywhere. Do you know how beautiful you are? You have the most beautiful blue eyes."

"I never had a looking glass to see myself. Thank you for the compliment."

"If you do not mind me asking, why did the both of you leave home?"

"All I will tell you is my parents were concerned about our safety. There were pogroms in our village, and they were killing girls of all ages. My mother has a sister living in America. Her sister said we would be safe in America. 'Send the girls to me.' That is all I will tell you. There is no more to the story."

"I am not too sure about that."

The waiter said, "Who gets the apple pie?"

Yankel said, "This lovely young lady."

"How did you get into acting and working in the theater?"

"I was born in Bucharest, and my parents owned this small theatre. They wanted the Jewish people to have some place to enjoy Yiddish plays. Acting has been in my family. It came naturally to me."

"How come you are living at Esther's?"

"It is near the theatre. I get my meals, and I have company at meals. It works for me."

"How did you get to Esther's?"

"This aunt in America and Esther were childhood friends. They corresponded with each other. Esther left for America before my aunt. She married a man from Bucharest and decided to stay. My aunt's husband went to America first. He then sent for her and the children. When she knew she was going to America, my aunt decided to stop in Bucharest and see her friend. Then they went on to America. She suggested we stop at Esther's house as she did before we continue to America. My aunt wrote to Esther. She agreed we stop at her place. We could see some of Europe before going to America." Sonia was getting into territory see wanted to stay away from. "Now you know a good bit of my life. This coffee is delicious. And the apple pie is good. Yankel, what is the next play you are showing?"

"Sonia, it is called producing a show."

"Oh!"

"You will learn all the words. Just give yourself time. Are you finished?"

"Yes."

"It is time we went home before your sister comes after me with a broom."

"Yes, I agree."

They left the coffee shop and proceeded to walk home. Each one was thinking their own thoughts.

Yankel asked, "Sonia, are you cold? Would you like my jacket?"

"Thank you. I am fine. I was just thinking how lucky Anna and I are meeting such caring and wonderful people." They started up the steps and into the house. "Thank you. This was an interesting experience. I had never been in a theatre before. I will speak with Anna and let you know tomorrow." Sonia started up the stairs to the third floor. "Anna, are you awake?"

"Yes, I was wondering what took you so long."

"After the show, Yankel and I stopped for dessert. He asked me if I would be the prompter for the shows. He said my Yiddish is good. The cast seemed to like me. I also think he likes me. If I take this job, we will not have to take any monies from the bank. He offered me twenty-five forint a week when the play is on. And he offered me fifteen a week when the cast is learning the parts."

"What does parts mean."

"The words they have to say while they are on the stage."

"Did you happen to say anything about me?"

"I will take you myself. I will arrange my schedule. I will go into class earlier. Then I will be able to come home sooner. Antoine will help me rearrange my schedule."

"Sonia, you sound like those college girls. It is late. Let's go to sleep. We will talk more in the morning."

"No. I am up. Tell me what you did after dinner."

"Sura and I played cards with Rabbi and Faygie."

"How many chips did you lose?"

"Not too many. This is the first time Rabbi played with us. He really knows his cards."

"Do you think Sura will be upset that I will be going to the theatre?"

"No, she has enough to do around the house. Esther keeps her busy. Now that I too am up, tell me exactly what you are doing."

"I am helping the cast—that is, the people in the play—learn their lines. I help them when they forget a word or a line while in front of the audience. The entire play is in Yiddish, and I do know Yiddish."

"What is the play about?"

"I do not know! I could not read the story. I was too busy keeping up with the words they were saying. I will be reading the story many times when they practice the play. You will come see the shows and not have to pay. Now please let's go to sleep. Love you."

"Love you too.'

In the morning, Anna said, "Sonia, get up. You have to go to the university, and I have to go to school. Please get dressed."

"All right. I will hurry."

"I want you to speak to Antoine today and change your courses. I would like to go see the family today."

"All right. I will meet you in the theatre this afternoon. I will talk to Antoine while we are on the streetcar. Let's get breakfast and be on our way."

Everyone was at the table when the girls walked into the dining room. The girls said good morning, rushed through breakfast, and were ready to travel.

Antoine said, "The both of you are really rushed."

"We did not want to be late."

Yankel and Anna rushed off. Antoine graded Sonia's books, and all were off to school.

Sonia confided in Antoine. She told him all about Anna wanting to work as a governess. She wanted to take Anna to her job and pick her up. She wanted to know what he thought. She knew she would have to change her class schedule. Would he help her? Sonia also told Antoine Yankel offered her the job as the prompter. Her Yiddish was perfect. She explained that they needed the money for their funds were getting low. Esther had asked her for weekly room-and-board money. The funds their father sent had run out.

Sonia also told Antoine, "There is money in the Bucharest bank that had been sent for the train tickets and the ship fare to America. The banker is going to arrange our travel arrangements when the time comes for the ships to be taking passengers." They talked about each problem.

Antoine asked, "Do you object to Anna working as a governess?"

"No, this would keep her busy."

Antoine thought the offer Yankel made was her answer to getting funds to live on while in Bucharest. Antoine said he definitely would help her change her classes if they were available. They would work together on the scheduling.

"We will work it out. When are you going to meet the family?"

"This afternoon."

"Are you comfortable doing this alone?"

"I think so. The advertisement in the paper said "governess to be taking care of two small girls, ages 4 and 6." The hours are from three till six, two days weekdays and all day Saturday from 10:00 a.m. till 6:00 p.m. My problem is I do not get out of school till 3:30 p.m. each day."

"Schedules are changed all the time. That is not difficult to change. Have we solved your problems?"

"Antoine, you are very easy to talk with."

"Thank you, Sonia."

We got off at the next stop.

Dora and the Banker

DORA COULD NOT STOP THINKING about Sonia and Anna. *How come Solomon, this important banker, is involved with two small girls from a small town in Ukraine? What family are they from? I must go and speak with Solomon. I must get some answers.* Dora walked into the bank and asked for Solomon Bally. She immediately was walked to his office.

"Good afternoon, Solomon. I am here to ask you a few questions."

"I know what you are going to ask. First, I must know. How did you meet these lovely young ladies?"

"I was waiting for the train to Bucharest at the Ungheni Prut station. I noticed a lady with two young girls. The girls were having their meal from a picnic basket which seemed unusual. We got on the train, and we were seated in the same car. The older woman got the girls settled in their seats and was talking to them. The conductor came through and said the train was departing in ten minutes. Then the strangest thing happened. The woman got off the train. She left the girls by themselves. I kept watching to see what they were doing. The train started to move. The older one, Sonia, approached me. She asked if I could tell her where the closet was. I said I had to go to the salon myself. I would take them. She said her sister had to use the facility. We went in the salon. Anna did not come out from the toilet for five minutes. I kept hearing the toilet flush time and time again. I asked, 'Are you all right?' She replied, 'I am watching the water go down the toilet. I do not know where it goes.' With that, I started to laugh to myself. I said, 'Come out, and I will explain it to you.' With that, she came out of the stall. She washed her hands, and I explained there are pipes beneath the toilet that take the water

125

away. 'Every time you flush, it takes the waste away and replaces it with clean water.' 'Oh!' she said. We finally left the salon. Sonia was frantic. She asked if everything was okay. We said yes.

"The girls thanked me. In a while, the both of them fell asleep. They woke up before we reached Bucharest. The two sisters had a discussion. The girls read until the conductor said 'Bucharest in ten minutes.' They packed their things and waited for the train to stop. Sonia again came and asked, 'Could you please direct us to where the carriage station would be? We are not familiar with this station.' I was busting. I wanted to know more about these children. I said, 'Follow me. I am going that way.' I got them a carriage. Sonia gave me a paper with their address to give to the driver, and I paid their fare. I also gave Sonia my card. I told her if I could help her, she has my address. I never heard from her, but I was going to look them up. The accidental meeting a few days ago was quite a surprise. Then when I heard they wanted to speak with you, I became curious. What did these children want from you?"

"I guess you were taken aback. Dora, I may need your help, so I will tell you the story."

Solomon told Dora about the pogroms and explained they were from a very small Jewish village. He explained the family was Jewish. "The girls would have been killed if their father had not hidden them for two days in the outhouse."

"Oh," said Dora. "Now I know about the toilet. I see. Their parents had to send them away."

"I do not know who helped them get out of Ukraine by crossing the ice river during the night or who picked them up on the other side of the river or how they got Romanian papers. We do not know who that lady was that put them on the train."

"We are not going to ask?"

"Albert told me that this has to be kept a secret. They are safe living with a family and friends. They got official papers to leave this country. I was told the girls must take this friend's daughter to America with them."

"Oh, what intrigue! If the girls were found, they could be sent back to Ukraine. People would be killed. Am I correct? How did you get involved Solomon?"

"There is a family that lived in the same town as the Zitefskys. This father knew his son was smart. He was aware his son wanted to go to the university. The family had no funds for university. The officials at the university told Albert's father that Albert could get into the university, but he needed tutorship fees. Albert's father knew of one person that may be able to help him. He went to talk to Mr. Zitefsky. He owned the only grocery store in Hajsyn. 'He allows the townspeople to take food and pay for it later. Maybe he could help us.'

"Mr. Lebad waited till all the customers left the shop. He said to Mr. Zitefsky, 'I have a problem. I was hoping you could help me.' He told Mr. Zitefsky the entire story. He then asked, 'Could you help us?' Mr. Zitefsky asked, 'What does your son want to study?' Mr. Lebad replied, 'When he leaves the university, he wants to be a banker.'

"Mr. Zitefsky offered, 'I will loan you the first two years fee for school. You can come and take all the food you need to live and any supplies you need for the two years. Can you then pay the university?' 'Yes!' replied Mr. Lebad. That is exactly what happened. Albert graduated, and his father paid back what he owed Mr. Zitefsky. Albert went on to not only get a job at the bank, he became part owner."

Dora said, "Mr. Zitefsky is a kind and caring person. I would like to meet him someday."

"Now that you know the story, we have to see that the girls become citizens of Romania."

"Not so fast, Solomon. How did you get to know Albert?"

"I needed funds to be delivered to a client in Podil. This was extremely important for my bank. I called the exchange in Podil and spoke with a few of the bankers at the bank. No one could help me. Finally, one banker connected me to the only banker who has the authority to make such a loan. They connected me to Albert. He told me, if I paid 1 percent higher than the lenders are paying, he would guarantee the money would be transferred into my client's account that day. I must pay the loan back with the extra interest in one week. Albert helped save my bank's reputation. I am indebted to him. Now back to the girls. Once they are citizens, they can go anywhere in the world."

"The other young lady, is she a citizen of Romania?"

"Yes, she was born here."

"Great, no problem there. We also must go to the American consulate. All the girls have to fill out an application for immigration visa (quota). It may take awhile to get that visa. When they get to America, they should become citizens of America. They will be safe there."

Solomon asked, "When could you start arrangements for the papers needed?"

"I can start and have them completed in two weeks."

"Really!" said Solomon.

"I am not a baroness for nothing."

"Good, I am looking at train schedules—Bucharest to Budapest to Zurich to Marseille. There is only one steamship line that goes to Philadelphia, Pennsylvania, and to Providence, Rhode Island. The aunt's name is Pessy Cohen. She lives at 902 Fifth Street, Philadelphia."

Dora said, "I think the girls should come and live with me until all the papers have been completed, even the application for entry into America."

"I agree. The young lady that was born here can stay at home. Once the papers are filled out and delivered to you, the girls can go back."

Dora thanked Solomon. "I will see the girls Sunday. I will let you know when we will meet."

The Circus

SONIA WAS ENJOYING HER BATH. She had been to the theatre for a few hours in the afternoon, helping the female lead learn the pronunciation of a few Jewish words.

Sonia said, "I never knew that Yiddish could be so hard to speak."

Anna said, "You never knew another language."

"That is true. Remember we are going to Dora's tomorrow."

"Sonia, do you still have her card? I would like to see the inside of her house," said Anna.

"It must be beautiful."

"I agree," said Anna. "What are you going to wear?"

"I have a dress with a full skirt. It has a beautiful belt with stones on it."

"Sounds good," Anna said. "I am wearing a plaid skirt and a brown blouse with full sleeves. Sonia, when are we going to go hat shopping? We have time."

"Wait till I work a few more weeks. We will then have some money to spend."

"You are right. I have to get out of this tub."

"Dinner will be ready soon."

"Will you go with me to see the children?"

"Yes."

"I want you to meet the family too."

"I definitely will go with you. Oh, Yankel said he will take you or pick you up when I cannot get there in time."

"Sonia, he likes you."

"Yes, I know."

"Let's see if anyone wants to go to the park for ice cream. I would like to wear my new walking shoes. I know Sura would like to go."

"I am telling you now, I will not go to the amusement park. I cannot go on the carousel."

"Okay, someone else will go with me. Are you ready, Sonia?"

"Yes."

"Would you brush my hair?"

"Yes, get your brush. Anna, you need some of your hair cut back. It is getting too long."

"Yes, I know."

"There goes that gong again. Let's start down the stairs."

They met Yankel on the way. It was Saturday night. They had cold chicken, noodles and cheese, potato pancakes.

"That is my best and donuts. Sonia, what are you going to drink tonight?"

"Hot tea."

"I thought you would be drinking coffee," teased Yankel.

"No, that is for eating with the cast."

We reached the dining room after everyone got there. The men stood up and helped us get seated. Dinner was on the center of the table. Everyone helped themselves. The servers offered tea and dessert.

Anna said, "Would anyone like to go to the fairgrounds for ice cream and walking? I have my walking shoes on."

To everyone's surprise, Rabbi and Faygie agreed to go. All seven of them got on the streetcar and were off to the fairgrounds. They were all surprised the fairgrounds were open and empty. This evening, there was a large white tent, with loud music coming from the tent.

There was a man standing on a ladder shouting, "Come to the circus. Come, see the clowns and the high-wire act. Come, see the elephants and the tigers. Come one, come all, to the circus. The circus starts in ten minutes."

They all decided this was something they must see. Sonia paid for herself and Anna. The rabbi paid for Faygie and himself. The boys paid for Sura. They went inside the tent. They found seats on the second row.

Sonia and Anna could not believe what they were seeing. There were three large rings in the middle of the tent. Clowns were running around on the floor of the tent and from ring to ring. Men came around selling popcorn and peanuts. The girls never saw such excitement. The lights were dimmed, and a man in a red coat came out.

He said, "Ladies and gentlemen, welcome to the circus of July 1917. Let the show begin!"

People and animals started to march from behind the tent. They went from one ring to another until the entire tent was full of animals, people, and clowns.

Sonia asked, "Yankel, those little people have white skin color. Is it their real color?"

"No, that is makeup, like what you have just started to wear. So you noticed?"

"Yes, I do."

"They are there to make people laugh. They do funny things. You will see."

The show started. Clowns were falling off the tigers. Beautiful ladies dressed in fancy colorful outfits were riding the elephants.

The announcer said, "The high wire will be performed by Alice and Buzzie. Ladies and gentlemen, keep your eyes in the sky."

The entire show lasted two hours. Sonia and Anna were so amazed they could not stop talking. The rabbi and Faygie could not believe people could fly in the sky. All in all, it was the most exciting evening had by all.

They were walking up the step to the house when Anna said, "We forgot to get ice cream."

Everyone said, "Good night."

Anna and Sonia said, "Thank you for a unforgettable evening. Good night."

"Sonia, I must write to the boys. They will definitely not believe what we saw this evening."

"I agree. I almost do not believe what we saw this evening. I wonder if there are things like this in America."

Dear Mama, Papa, Sol, Lou, and Reba,

Sonia and I just came from the fairgrounds in one of the large parks in the city. We had to tell you all about it. You will not believe what we saw tonight. It is called a circus where people, elephants, tigers, and little people with white faces perform.

This evening, there was a large white tent, with loud music coming from the tent. There was a man standing on a ladder shouting, "Come to the circus. Come, see the clowns and the high-wire act. Come, see the elephants and the tigers. Come one, come all to the circus."

The rabbi, his wife, the other Sonya, Yankel, and Antoine also went into the tent to see the show. There were three large rings in the middle of the tent. Clowns were running around the floor, jumping and falling over each other. Men came around selling popcorn and peanuts. A man in a red coat came out. He said, "Ladies and gentlemen, welcome to the circus. Let the show begin!"

People and animals started to march from behind the tent. They went from one ring to another until the entire tent was full of animals, people, and clowns. Clowns were falling off the tigers. Beautiful ladies dressed in fancy colorful outfits were riding the elephants.

The announcer said, "The high wire will be performed by Alice and Buzzie. Ladies and gentlemen, keep your eyes in the sky."

A man and a woman appeared from the top of the tent. They started flying from a wire and a swing. The entire show lasted two hours. Sonia and I still cannot believe what we saw.

I said I must write to Sol and Lou. They would never believe what we saw tonight. We want you to see this when you come to America.

We wonder if Reba got her shoes? We sent two sizes, one for now and one for later. Does Reba like her new doll? It has a name. She is called Raggie Ann.

How is Papa's leg? Can he walk? There is no war in Bucharest or any part of Romania. I was told that we are a neutral county. Sonia's letter is here as well.

Love you, Anna

Dear Papa, Mama, Sol, Lou, and Reba,

Anna and I went to the bank. The banker's name is Solomon Bally. He seems to be a good friend of Albert's. He is going to make all the arrangements for us to travel after the war to France. He is looking for a ship that goes directly into Philadelphia. Tell Mama to write to her sister in Philadelphia. We will write to her when we arrive in Marseille, France. We will tell her what ship we are on and the date of arrival. We are not sure when we will be able to go to Philadelphia. It depends on what is happening with this war.

I am working in the Yiddish theatre. This is a building in which people are seated and watch people perform on a stage. The people performing are called actors. I am there to help the actors speak Yiddish properly, and if they forget what to say, I help them. Mama, you would love the theater. I am making good money. It is enough to pay Esther weekly and have money for the university. Anna is looking for a job watching children. She is good at that. We just got home from the circus.

I am tired. I will write more next time.

Love and kisses, Sonia

The Luncheon

"ANNA, WAKE UP. WE MUST get ready. We are going to lunch at Dora's house. I do not want to be late."

"Neither do I, Sonia. I am up."

"Let's go a little earlier. I am not sure if we are supposed to bring a gift. Let's stop at the apothecary shop and see if we can buy her something. I do not want to look like a greenhorn."

"Sonia, where did you learn that word?"

"At the theatre."

"What does it mean?"

"A person who is in a new country and does not know anything about the country or the language."

"Were we greenhorns?"

"Yes."

"Ugh."

"But now we know French, Yiddish, and English. What are we called now?"

"I do not know, and I am not going to ask."

"Are you dressed? Did you tell Esther that we are only having tea and a muffin? Did you tell her that we are invited to lunch?"

"I will announce it when we go downstairs."

They entered the dining room. The rabbi and Faygie were finishing their breakfast.

They asked, "Where is everyone?"

"Not too sure," said Faygie.

Esther came out from the kitchen.

Anna said, "We have been invited for lunch. We met this woman on the train. She helped us with getting a carriage to come here. She even paid our fare."

"Anna and I saw her again when we were getting baby shoes at the apothecary shop. She lives around the corner in one of those fancy houses." Sonia said, "I have her card."

"What is her name?" Faygie asked.

"Dora Farket."

"What did you say? Please, may I see her card?" said Esther. "Girls, tell me again how you met her."

"She was on the train with us. We were not sure where to get the carriages, so I asked her for help. She was nice and took us right to the carriage station. She gave the driver our address and paid our fare. We met again in the apothecary shop. We started to talk. She invited us for lunch."

"Young ladies, you really are something. You just met Baroness Doris Farket. Her husband was distantly related to King Ferdinand. She is quite a lady. You never know who you are going to meet on the train."

"We want to know. Should we bring something for her?"

"That would be nice. Try perfume."

"What is perfume?"

"It is fancy smelling water," said Faygie. "Go into the apothecary shop. They may have something for you."

"Anna, we better start out now. We have shopping to do."

The girls got the next streetcar. They knew exactly where to get off. They entered the apothecary shop.

Anna asked the salesperson, "Do you have any perfume?"

"Yes, we do. Which one would you like?"

"Can we smell them."

"Definitely."

The salesperson opened a few bottles. The girls were confused. They were smelling too many different fragrances.

Sonia said, "Can you help us? This is for Baroness Doris Farket."

"Oh, I know the one she likes. I have it right here."

"How much is it?"

"Five forints."

"That is expensive."

"Maybe you would like a scarf instead."

136

"No, we will take the perfume."

"Could you please wrap it?"

The girls were at Dora's door. Anna pulled the bell. A very nice man answered the door.

He said, "Good afternoon, ladies. Please come in. The baroness will be down shortly. May I take your package?"

"No, we will hold it."

He turned and left. Shortly, Dora walked into the room.

Anna said, "Dora we brought you a small gift. This is to thank you for all your help and for paying the fare to the carriage driver."

Dora said, "I was concerned you did not have the correct money or the correct fare for the driver." Dora opened the package and was pleasantly surprised at the gift. "Girls, this is lovely. Thank you. Shall we have lunch outside?"

"Yes, please," said Sonia.

Lunch was interesting and very fancy. They did have ice cream for dessert.

Dora said, "Girls, we have to talk. Please come into my study."

They followed Dora into this beautiful room lined with books of all kinds. There was a small sofa and a few sitting chairs near a window. She suggested they sit on the sofa.

Dora said, "By now, you know that Solomon Bally is a friend of mine as well as my banker. He told me your entire story. I must say I am very proud of you. I am going to help get you to America."

The Move to Dora's House

"This is what Mr. Bally and I planned. We hope you understand there is a war going on. We are not in it as yet. We must work fast before Romania get involved. You both have to become citizens of Romania. You can never apply for a visa to go to America or anywhere out of Romania. Next, you have to establish an address where you live and how long have you been here.

"I want you to both come live with me for two weeks. You move in with your valise and books and miscellaneous items. You can go back to Esther's after we have all the official papers signed. I do not want to interrupt your daily life. You will go to school, see your friends, and do all your daily chores. After you get your citizenship papers, you are free to go out of Romania. You just have to show your papers. If anyone asks you, tell them you are a citizen of Romania. Do not say Ukraine. You must forget about Ukraine, especially when you are in France and on the ship.

"We must request an application for an immigration visa. I just was informed there is a quota to get into America. This is due to the war."

"Where do we go for that?" asked Anna.

"We go to the American consulate. There I can help you. I will use my influence to speed up the visa application. I hope I will not have trouble with the quota. Remember you came out of Ukraine illegally. You had no papers. Someone got papers for you. That is how you got on the train to Bucharest. They went through a lot of trouble. Now that you are here, you need papers to leave here and go on your way to America. Solomon and I want to help you. I think you and Anna are the bravest young ladies I have ever met. I am proud to know you. If I may ask, how did you get out of Ukraine?"

"We are sorry. We can never tell. We promised our father we would never tell. We walked across a frozen river during the night. We cannot tell you anymore. We are just happy that we are alive."

Dora said, "I'm going to see that you get to America. You went such a long way alone, trusting strangers with your life. I must say your father must be a wonderful man, knowing that the both of you will be taken care of by strangers/friends. He must have done something for the people that took care of you on your travels to Bucharest."

"Dora, our father is a caring man. He has helped the townspeople, like Albert and his family. When the townspeople needed help, he was always there. I never knew how much till now."

"When are we meeting again. We would like to get our Romanian citizenship papers. That would be one less thing we have to be concerned about, especially with war all around us."

Dora said, "You will have those papers in two weeks. First, I need your full names and the correct spelling. I am using my address. If asked, you are my sister-in-law's grandchildren. You have come to stay with me because there is fighting in Budapest. Why not move in next Friday? You can move in and unpack. We can go shopping Saturday in the Lipscani neighborhood."

Sonia said, "I must be at work Sunday after dinner. The rest is fine with us."

Anna asked, "Is there a hat shop in that area? I hope so. I love trying on hats."

"I forgot to tell you. Sonya Trager was born here. She will have no problems. She just needs her birth certificate. She is a citizen by birth. When we are ready to go for the visas, she will have no problems."

"When do we meet with Mr. Bally?"

"What does the bank and Solomon Bally have that belongs to you?"

Anna laughed. "Money. We do not know how much our father has been putting in the bank for us. We do not know if he still is sending money through Albert and his bank."

"We were hoping Mr. Bally would give us those answers. That is why we want to go back and meet with him again. We will need money for train tickets, lodging, and food. What I make is fine for us now, but not for a long time."

"Do you mind if I go back with you to meet Solomon Bally?" asked Dora.

"No, we would love that. Anna or I are not the aware of the money exchange and the names of the notes and coins."

"I know what you are talking about. It took me a long time to learn the currency. We will move in Friday afternoon."

"I thought you were born in Bucharest," said Sonia.

"No, I am originally from Budapest."

"Dora, I wrote to my father that I have a job. We have not taken any money out of the bank in Podil or in Bucharest. Anna and I do not want him to send any more money. We used all the coins that were sewn in our clothes. We still have the gold necklaces around our necks."

"Girls, are you telling me that your mother and you were sewing coins into your clothes? How did you walk?"

Sonia said, "Very slowly and carefully."

"Do you have the necklaces on now."

Both of them said, "Yes!"

"How did you expect to exchange them?"

"We were going to exchange them in France a section at a time."

"Can they do that for you or anyone?"

"We are not sure."

Dora said, "Let's talk about that later. Sonia, you have to go work. Where are you working?"

"At the Jewish theater. I am the prompter. The shows are in Yiddish. That is all we spoke at home."

"That is wonderful."

"May I ask what you are getting?"

"I am getting twenty-five forints a week when there is a show. I am getting fifteen forints when there is no show, but I am helping the actors with the words. Anna is getting a position being a governess to a few small children. She is going for an interview Monday afternoon."

"Ladies, I too have some place to go tonight. I will see you next Friday. Let me know if you get the position."

"We will, Dora. Thank you again. We will see you next Friday."

The girls ran for the streetcar that had just stopped. The conductor waited for them. Anna started to say something, but Sonia stopped her.

Sonia said, "Let's wait till we get home."

They finished the ride, each thinking her own thoughts.

The girls no sooner walked in the door when Esther asked, "How was your afternoon?"

When everyone heard the girls were home, they came into the sitting room.

"What type of a person is the baroness?"

"Let's see now," Anna started. "She wore a gown with a red sash across her chest. She had a diamond tiara in her hair and beautiful rings on her fingers. There was a butler and three serving maids."

"What else was there, Sonia?"

"The inside of the house was beautiful. The bathroom sinks were made of gold."

"Come on now. What was she really like?"

"First, I think we should tell you how we met Dora. She was on the same train going to Bucharest. We did not know anything about bathrooms, transportation, carriages, or streetcars. We saw this lovely lady sitting by herself. Anna had to go to the bathroom. I went and asked her where the toilets were. She replied, 'I have to go there myself. I will show her.' They came back fifteen minutes later. I asked, 'Anna, what happened?' Anna started to tell me about the toilets flushing, and she kept on flushing, wondering where the waste water was going. Dora was intrigued with Anna's reaction to the toilet. Then when the conductor announced 'Bucharest in ten minutes,' Anna was concerned we would not know where to go when we got off the train. I again went to this woman and asked her if she could tell me where I could get transportation to my aunt's house. I gave her Esther's address. She nicely said, 'I am going that way. Follow me.' That was comforting for Anna and me. We all got off the train together, and we followed her. She took us right to the carriages. She told the driver our address and even paid our fare. Dora gave me her card. She said if we need some further assistance, we were to call her. We happened to meet her again in the apothecary store when buying Reba's shoes. That was when we were invited for lunch."

Yankel said, "Sonia, we have to go. There is a show tonight. The house is sold out."

Anna said, "What is a sold-out house?"

Sonia said, "All the tickets to see the show were purchased."

"Oh."

Yankel and Sonia left. The rest of the family decided to play cards.

On the way to the theater, Yankel said, "Well, you learn fast, my sophisticated young lady. What really happened with the baroness?"

"I will tell you later. It is rather complicated."

The show ended; the audience applauded. The curtain came down, and the cast walked out. Yankel locked up, then they walked out of the theater.

"Do you want to go for coffee?"

"No. What I have to tell I cannot say with people around us. It is for your ears only." They were in front of the house. "Let's sit outside on the steps. The story Anna and I told this afternoon is true. We met Dora on the train. She kept looking at us and wondering what adult would put two children on a train and then leave. She was so happy when I asked her for help. We did not see each other till two weeks ago at the Bucharest bank. Our father had sent money for our fare to America and the trains to get to Marseille.

"I cannot tell you how we got to Bucharest. We will never be able to tell that story till my entire family is safe in America. The baroness is helping us become citizens. Anna and I have to go there to live for a time. We have to prove we are residents. We are going to use her address until all the papers are completed. We must work fast before Romania gets involved in the war. That is why she is helping us to get our citizenship papers. Once we have those papers, we can go to the American consulate. The next thing we have to do is fill out an application for a visa to America. I have one more thing to tell you. Sonya Trager is going with us. No one knows this."

"Wow! I never expected a story like that. Well, if Romania goes to war, I will be drafted in the army."

"Yankel, promise me you will not tell anyone. I am so grateful for the job at the theater. You have been so kind to Anna and me."

"Sonia, I do like you."

"I like you too, Yankel. We will not be coming to Esther's. We will be staying at Dora's for the two weeks. We will be doing our everyday activities. When all the papers are completed, we will be back at Esther's."

"Sonia, I promise I will never say anything. We never even talked."

"Thank you, Yankel. I am tired. It is my bedtime."

"Sonia, I admire you. Good night.'

"Anna, are you up?"

"How did the show go?"

"Fine. It is really fun. We have to talk. We have to tell Esther what we have to do in order to get our Romanian papers. We are grateful we met Dora. We may have been here for three or four more years till we got papers."

"I think Solomon will have been able to get papers for us as well. It would have just taken longer."

"Anna, I am very tired. Good night. Love you."

"Love you too."

The days rushed by. Anna and Sonia went to the house of Mr. and Mrs. Karl Stefan. Anna met with their two lovely daughters. They hired Anna on the spot. They were paying three forints during the week. She would get five forints on Saturdays. The girls explained they had a previous engagement. Anna would not be able to come that Saturday. It would have to start the following week. They agreed to this arrangement.

The next week flew by. The girls had to move to Dora's house. They took one valise and filled it with a few lovely dresses and their walking shoes.

They arrived at Dora's at 3:00 p.m. The butler showed them in and announced them to Dora. She was happy to see the girls. She wanted to know if they enjoyed the train ride. She asked one of the maids to show them to their rooms. The routine at Dora's house was much different. She did have a butler and a few maids. The help was at the girls' side all the time. They excused themselves to unpack. Dora said she would meet them in the library.

Anna and Sonia said, "That would be fine."

They were amazed at what they saw. There were two adjoining bedrooms with a salon in-between.

The maid asked, "Are these rooms satisfactory?"

They replied, "Yes, they are lovely."

They unpacked their dresses, put a few items away, and started down the stairs. The butler was waiting for them at the bottom of the stairs.

"The baroness is waiting for you in the library."

They walked into the library. Dora closed the door. She asked them to sit down.

"I have good news for you. I have agents working on your citizenship papers. Hopefully they will be done next week. The bad news is you will have to stay here for the full two weeks. The staff has too many eyes and ears."

"We understand."

Sonia said, "I think we could stay here longer. I hope we will not be a burden for you and the staff."

"I will love it," said Dora. "My children are busy and do not come often. I have two daughters. You are using their rooms."

"The rooms are beautiful."

Anna said, "You have an interesting library."

"Girls, while you are here, feel free to make this your home."

Both girls said, "Thank you."

"I told the staff that you are my sister-in-law's grandchildren from Budapest. You are passing through for a week or two. I offered you the use of my house for your stay. That is all the staff needs to know."

We walked in her beautiful garden and enjoyed sitting outside.

The butler came out and said, "Is there anything I could get for you?"

Dora said, "A pot of tea, girls?"

"Yes," said Anna.

Dora said, "And some cookies, if we have any."

"Yes, the chef made some just today."

Dora said, "Dinner is served at 7:00 p.m. The chef has fish on Friday."

"That is fine with Anna and me. We are not fancy eaters."

Anna asked, "Does he serve ice cream?"

"Let's talk about tomorrow."

"Yes," said Anna. "Tell us about Lipscani area."

"Back in the 1400s, most merchants and craftsmen established their stores and shops in a particular section of the city. This area became known for the many German traders from Lipsca. Other streets took the names of other crafts such as furrier (banan), shoe-makers (cavafil vechil). The area was and is called Lipscani. It is a very large shopping area."

Anna asked, "Is there a hat shop?"

"Yes!"

"Girls, we will invade this area tomorrow."

The butler brought out the afternoon tea and cookie. He served the tea. The three of them enjoyed the beautiful afternoon and the tea.

Sonia thought to herself, *This is the first time I have really relaxed outside of a hot bath.* "Dora, tell us about your daughters."

"The girls are twins and are married. I have two grandsons, one boy from each daughter."

"When was the last time you saw them."

"I was coming from visiting them when I saw the two of you on the train."

The butler appeared at the doorway. "Excuse me. There is gentleman here to see you."

"Ask him to join us in the garden."

To Sonia and Anna's surprise, Solomon Bally appeared in the doorway. Dora greeted him and asked him to sit with them.

Dora said to the butler, "There will be another person for dinner."

"Yes, ma'am."

"Would you please get Mr. Bally his usual drink. Now, ladies, we can have a small family dinner."

Anna was too surprised to talk. Sonia squeaked out, "That is nice."

Dora explained, "If you remembered, I told you Mr. Bally and I are friends. He comes often for dinner. Now if you both take your surprised look off your faces. We can have our discussion here instead of the bank. We can talk freely here."

Solomon thanked the butler for his drink.

Solomon said, "I have wonderful news for you, Sonia and Anna. I have with me your Romanian citizenship papers. I was surprised they came so early. They were delivered to me late this afternoon. We had a rush put on your papers. I have some bad news. Romania is going to be at war in the next few weeks. Romania is joining forces with America, Great Britain, France, Russia, and Italy. We are hoping this war will be over quickly. I am sorry to say you cannot travel. You will have to sit the war out in Bucharest."

Sonia said, "I know worst places we could be."

"You must go to the American consulate to put in your request for an application for an immigration visa. I was informed there will soon be a quota of people allowed in America. Girls, you will have to go first thing Monday morning and apply for a visa. You will have to see how the consulate responds to your request. Show the official at the consulate your Romanian papers. Tell them you have family in America. If they ask who in America you are going to visit, give them your aunt's name, street address in Philadelphia, Pennsylvania."

Dora asked, "Can I go with them?"

"No, we may need you if we have a problem later. I will have one of my people take them to the consulate. She will meet you here Monday morning 10:00 a.m. sharp."

The butler came out with a second drink for Solomon just as he finished the first. Sonia noted he seemed to be more than a friend.

Solomon said, "I have some spending money for the both of you. I was not sure of your money situation. I know you are going with Dora to shop. I decided to bring you some extra spending money. I also have a complete file with me of the money that was put into your account."

"How much is still there."

"The only money taken out of your account is what I am giving you today. I have a listing of what it will cost for the ship and traveling expenses. Look it over with Dora."

Sonia and Anna said, "Thank you, Solomon. You are a true friend."

"Dora and I think you are the bravest young ladies we have ever met."

Sonia asked, "Are the men going to be told they have to join the army?"

"Only if the actual fighting comes in to Romania. We have a large reserve army. Let's hope, with America in the fight, the war will soon be over."

Dora said, "Let's forget everything outside these four walls."

A wonderful dinner had been prepared for them. The butler came out to the garden and announced, "Dinner is served."

The girls never dined in such splendor like they did that evening. The dessert was strawberries on top of a yellow cake covered with ice cream and fluffy, thick white cream sauce. After dinner, they went into the library.

Solomon asked, "Girls, do you play cards?"

"Yes, only some games."

"What do you play?"

"Poker."

"Really?" said Dora. "Who taught you that?"

"I learned it at the theater."

"Dora, get the chips out. We will play a while. Girls, are you all right with that?"

"Yes."

The chips were distributed. The game began. They all had a wonderful evening.

Dora said, "This is the last hand."

Everyone agreed. The cards and chip were put away. Anna and Sonia thanked both Dora and Solomon for all they were doing for them. They climbed the stairs and went into a bedroom.

Anna said, "Pick your bed."

"Anna, they are both are the same. I will take the other room."

"First, I want to look at the papers Solomon gave us."

Sonia opened the booklet. The girls stared at the figures on the paper. They saw numbers but really did not understand them.

"We will have to ask Dora to explain these figures. I will take this file and put it into the valise. We will talk to Dora in the morning."

Both girls fell into bed and were fast asleep. Anna woke up and decided to take her bath, then wake Sonia. She had finished dressing when Sonia came into her room.

"How would you like to live like Dora?"

"I would have to find a baron."

"Right now I am looking for the good-looking, tall, dark-haired boy that walks down our street."

"If it is meant to be, Anna, you will see him again."

"Let's talk about the things we want to do and buy. We can buy the boys a cap like Leon's."

"Reba is easy, a talking doll."

"Papa could use a pretty sweater with a zipper. Mama could use a new dress or shawl and maybe a hat."

"We have an entire day to shop and walk. Put your walking shoes on."

"Sonia, are you dressed?"

"Yes."

The girls entered the dining room. Dora was already seated and having her tea.

"Good morning, Dora," the girls said.

The butler appeared and asked the girls what they would like to drink.

Both answered, "Tea."

What happened next surprised the girls. From the kitchen came two ladies carrying trays of food.

"Dora, thank you, but Anna and I could not possibly eat all this food."

"I know. I was not sure what you would like. I promise, tomorrow Hans will ask you what you would like for breakfast."

"Anna, we will have to do a lot of walking to walk off all this food."

Breakfast was finished, and the three girls went shopping. Anna insisted Dora try the streetcar, instead of her car.

"I will pay the fare."

They all walked to the station and took the streetcar to the Lipscani area. There were all kinds of shops, more than the girls ever thought existed. The three of them went from shop to shop up one side of the street down the other.

Dora finally said, "Girls, I am going to sit at this café and have a cup of tea. When you are ready for lunch, meet me here."

The girls went on their way to view and visit more shops.

"Good afternoon, ladies. Can I help you?"

"We are interested in trying on one of your coats."

"Of course," said the lady in the shop. "Which one are you interested in trying on."

Sonia said, "The one with the brown soft fur."

"The beaver coat."

"Yes."

"I am not sure I have your size. I will look in the stock room."

The lady came out with a lovely brown coat but not the one Sonia wanted. The lady put the coat on Sonia.

"This is a mink skin coat."

"Oh, this is beautiful. How much is this?"

"I will look in the ledger to see the price."

"I am just looking now."

Anna decided not to try on coats. They thanked the lady and left.

Sonia said, "Someday I will get one of those coats."

Both girls laughed. The girls purchased two outfits for Reba, a shawl for their mother, and a sweater for their father. They waited to go to the hat shop for caps for the boys.

"Anna, do you think we should get Dora a hat while we are in the shop?"

"Good idea, Sonia."

They went back to the café.

"There you are, ladies! I was wondering what happened to the both of you."

"We went into a shop that had fur coats."

"Well, you picked a nice shop to visit. Are you ready for lunch?"

They ordered lunch and tea. Sonia ordered coffee. Both Anna and Dora looked at her.

"I have lunch with the cast, and they all drink coffee."

Dora paid the bill, and they went to shop again. They looked for a hat shop.

Dora said, "My milliner is a block away. Would you like to go there? They may have boy's caps."

As they entered the shop, a salesclerk addressed Dora, "Good afternoon, Baroness. May I help you?"

"Yes, I have my sister's granddaughters staying with me. They are interested in boy's caps."

"I have men's caps. The smaller size will fit them."

"The girls are also interested in a hat. Can you help them?"

"Of course."

"Girls, look around and see if there is a hat you would like."

Sonia saw just what she wanted, a lovely red hat with a wide brim and a flower. Anna saw a brown cloche that matched her eyes.

The clerk asked Dora, "Are you purchasing a hat today?"

"Not really."

The girls insisted she try some hats on. The sales clerk brought out this lovely pink hat with a pink flower and surrounded with lots of pink ribbon around the brim of the hat.

"The hat is just made for you, Dora."

The girls informed the sales clerk, "Please box that hat along with the other two hats."

The sales clerk brought out two caps that would fit the boys. They asked her to wrap them as well. They all walked out of the shop with a hat box.

"Girls, this was a surprise. Thank you."

"Dora, we could never repay you for all that you have done for us."

When they finally reached the house, they dropped the packages and needed to remove their shoes.

Dora said, "Thank you for a wonderful day and this beautiful hat."

The butler asked, "What time would you like dinner?"

Dora replied, "We would like a light dinner at seven."

In the evening, we showed Dora all the gifts we got for our family. Again Dora wondered how their family was going to get these packages. She never asked. Dora and the girls enjoyed the remainder of the evening in the garden.

Dora asked, "What are you going to do in America?"

Sonia answered, "I am going to work. Anna and I are both going to work and save money to bring our family to America. The situation in Ukraine is not good. My father is lucky he has the grocery shop, and the people know him and protect our family. We are going to leave as much money in Solomon's bank as possible so our family can use it to get to America."

"Where are you going to live once you arrive in America?"

"My aunt has lived in America for twenty years. She is expecting us. Of course, with the war on, no one can tell when people will be able to travel again. The army has the use of all the ships. We will have to wait till the war is over. Dora, do you think we will have fighting in Bucharest."

"I do not think so. The fighting seems to be closer to Germany."

"Dora, do you know anything about acquiring a visa?"

"I only know it is good for a year in America. That is from the time you set foot in America. Solomon is sending a specialist. She will help you in filling out the papers and answering the question. Let her do most of the talking. She will guide the both of you through this question period. Girls, I am not sure how long this visa process is going to take. You both are welcome here. Stay as long as you must. I, for one, do enjoy your company."

The girls said, "Thank you. Dora, we hope you enjoy your hat. We did not know what sort of thank-you gift we could give you."

"Girls, I never would have bought myself a pink hat. It is beautiful, and I do look good in it."

The butler came into the garden and asked if they wanted anything.

Anna and Sonia said, "No, thank you."

Dora said, "Maybe later."

"We have a big day tomorrow. Good night, Dora."

"Good night, girls. Sonia, when the young lady from the bank comes, feel free to use the library. I hope all goes well tomorrow."

"Thank you."

The girls had trouble sleeping. Anna said, "Can I sleep with you tonight?"

"Yes."

Sonia was thinking about home. She missed her papa. He would always know what to say when she was frightened. Tonight, she was frightened.

Early the next day, Sonia was up, had her bath, and was dressed before Anna was awake. She then woke Anna.

"Get up. It is a big day today."

With that, Anna jumped out of Sonia's bed and fell down. "I forgot I was sleeping with you."

"Are you hurt?"

"No." Anna took a quick bath, got dressed, and was ready to go downstairs with Sonia.

The girls were just about to say good morning to Dora, but she was not in the room. The butler came into the dining room.

He asked, "What would you like for breakfast?"

"Two muffins each and a pot of hot tea. Is Dora joining us for breakfast?"

"No, she is sleeping in this morning. She left a message. She will see you late this afternoon.'

The door pull rang just as the girls finished eating.

The butler announced, "There is a young lady at the door asking for Sonia."

"Yes, we are expecting her. Please let her in. Dora said we can use the library."

"I am aware."

"Thank you."

"My name is Rachel. I am going to do most of the talking. You will be going through an interview. You will answer the questions truthfully. Sonia, how old are you?"

"Sixteen."

"When is your birthday?"

"May 10."

"Anna, how old are you?"

"Fourteen."

"When is your birthday?"

"June 15."

"Why are you going to America?"

"To visit my aunt in America."

"The questions will be like that. Remember you are a Romanian citizen. Show him your papers. Solomon sent birth certificates with the date of your birth and names of your mother and father."

Sonia looked at hers. "How did he get this information?"

"From Albert. I do not think he will ask many questions from Anna. Anna, you just show him your birth certificate and citizenship papers. Remember, I will do most of the talking. Do you have any questions?"

"What if they ask where we were born?"

"They will not ask that question. You have a birth certificate. Stop worrying. I am there to help you. Shall we go, ladies. We cannot be late."

The US embassy was not far from Dora's house. Rachel decided they should walk the seven blocks. The embassy was not a fancy building. There was a large sign over the doorway saying "US Embassy." We entered the building and a sign said "US visa to the left." We went down the hall to a door that read "US Consular Office." Rachel went up to the desk.

She said, "I am here with Anna and Sonia Zitefsky. They are requesting a visa to visit America."

"You do know there is a war going on. Do you have an appointment?"

"Yes. Here is my business card."

"I will take it into the consular officer."

The assistant came back. She said, "He will be with you shortly."

Rachel said, "Thank you." And we all sat down to wait.

A half hour later, a man came out of the room. He apologized for keeping us waiting. He asked us to come into his office. He told us to sit next to his desk.

Rachel started by saying, "I have two young ladies that want to visit their aunt in America. They need visas. I have their birth certificates and their citizenship papers."

Rachel placed them on his desk. He looked at them and handed them back to Rachel.

"Tell me, ladies, where are you going in America?"

Sonia answered, "We are going to Philadelphia."

"Do you know where Philadelphia is in America?"

"We were told it is in the state of Pennsylvania."

"Do you have the address where you are going?"

"Yes. 502 South Fifth Street."

"I was in Philadelphia one time. That is in South Phila. Ladies, here is what I am going to do for you. You will not be able to travel to America till the war is over. I will issue the both of you a non-quota visa. The maximum stay is one year from the day you set foot in America. The cost is two American dollars for immediate service."

Rachel said, "I will pay the two dollars. Where do we go?"

"Down the hall. It will say 'Cashier.' You will get a receipt. You will pick up the visa tomorrow after 2:00 p.m. at the cashier's window."

Anna and Sonia said, "Thank you."

The girls followed Rachel to the cashier's window. She paid the two dollars, and the three of them left. They walked back to Dora's house.

Rachel said, "That was not that bad."

"Not bad at all. Thanks to you. My sister and I appreciate your help."

"Someone will bring the visa to Dora's house. I am going to leave you. I must get back to work."

"Thank you again."

Anna pulled the bell, and the butler opened the door.

Dora was nowhere to be found. The girls went into their rooms, sat down on a bed, and started to cry.

"Anna, if it were not for Dora and Solomon, we would never have gotten out of Bucharest."

"What are we going to say to Sonya?"

"She has the papers we have. She is to go into the embassy and ask for the same visa we have. She must do it tomorrow. I have a show tonight. I will give her all the information Rachel left. Anna, can you believe we are going to America?"

The girls washed their faces and went downstairs looking for Dora. The butler informed them Dora would be back by 3:00 p.m.

Anna said, "I am glad I did not have to start work today."

"I have to work tonight. I must be there by 7:30 p.m. The show starts at 8:30 p.m."

"Sonia, what are we going to tell Dora?"

"Let's leave a note for Dora, tell her we will be back for dinner."

The library door opened, and Dora walked in. The girls ran, hugged her, and kissed her.

"We cannot thank you enough. We would never have gotten the papers if not for you."

"When do you get the visas?"

"Rachel will bring the papers here tomorrow."

"Girls, that is wonderful."

"The official said it is better that we do not leave the country. The visa is good for a year in America."

"Girls, I was just at the telegraph office. My girls wrote that the fighting maybe coming to Budapest. They fear for themselves and the children. I just sent a telegram to them to take the next train to Bucharest. It leaves Budapest at 8:00 p.m. and arrives at 8:00 a.m. My family will be here tomorrow morning. I must ask you—"

"Dora, we understand. We will leave this afternoon."

"Girls, let's have a celebration lunch before you leave."

"That would be lovely."

The girls told Dora everything that happened. "We get our papers tomorrow."

The butler announced lunch. They talked through lunch. The girls went upstairs and packed.

When they came down, the butler said, "The baroness is waiting for you in the library."

"Girls, I am very happy that you got your visas. I feel badly that we did not have more time together."

Sonia put her arms around Dora. "We understand. Just think, Dora, you will have your family together. We know they will arrive safely. Don't worry."

"Thank you. Girls, you will have to go to the bank tomorrow. Solomon will have your visas."

"Dora, thank you again for all you have done for us."

"Girls, keep in touch, I want to know how you are doing."

"We will." Anna and Sonia kissed her and left.

The girls walked slowly to the streetcar. They felt badly for Dora.

"I hope Dora's family will arrive safely."

"So do I, Sonia."

They got on the streetcar. Neither said anything on the way to Esther's. The girls walked to the house and up the stairs to the room.

Sura followed them upstairs. "Did everything go as planned?"

"Yes, we get our visas tomorrow. I have a package for you. We had a woman go with us to get our visas. She was wonderful. You will have no problem. You were born here. Just bring you birth certificate."

"What is in the package?"

"Open it."

"There is a note and two one-dollar American bills."

"That is the cost of the visa. You must have American money. That must have come from Dora. She thinks of everything. You better go tomorrow. They are going to stop issuing visas."

"Thank you, girls. I appreciate your help."

Both girls were tired. Anna took a bath. Sonia fell fast asleep. Anna woke Sonia up. It was almost time for dinner.

"I am not hungry. I really want to sleep."

"You have a job, remember?"

"Oh, yes. I am up."

"Are you ready to go downstairs?"

"Yes, let's go."

They started down the stairs and met Antoine on the way.

"Where were you, ladies?"

"We will tell you all about it at dinner."

The gong went off. Dinner was ready. After they were all seated, the questions started.

Sonia said, "It is very simple. We were at Dora's. She was helping us get our visas. We slept there for this agent was picking us up at her house. She took us to the US embassy. We have to pick up our visas tomorrow. That is the story. We were told we should not try to go anywhere because of the war."

Esther said, "Can we eat now?"

Yankel came in late. He said, "Sonia, I am so glad to see you. We have to leave at 7:30 p.m. today."

"I will be ready."

Yankel and Sonia went to the theater. Faygie got the cards out, and they had an enjoyable game.

Yankel wanted to know if all was okay.

"Yes, we were lucky to get our visas when we did. The embassy will close and not give out visas till after the war. Sonya will go tomorrow to the embassy. As soon as the show is over, I am going to sleep."

Meanwhile, when the card game ended, Esther said, "Anna, can I see you?"

"Yes."

Esther asked, "Do you have all your papers?"

"Yes, and our visas, we will pick them up tomorrow."

"Are you going with Sonya tomorrow."

"She has all the instructions and the two American dollars."

"What is that for?" asked Esther.

"It costs two dollars for the visa. Ask Sonya. She will show you the instructions."

Sonia and Yankel came in. Sonia went directly to bed.

The girls slept through the gong. There was no hurry. The visas would not be at the bank till after noon. Esther and Sonya left for the US embassy. The girls found their way to the bank. They again met the man in the red coat.

"Mr. Bally please."

"Sorry, he is busy."

Sonia had just about lost her temper when she remembered the card in her purse. She pulled out the card. She showed it to the man. He moved quickly. He showed the girls to Solomon's office. Solomon waved his hand for them to enter. He motioned for them to be seated. He was talking to someone.

"How are you, young ladies?"

"Very well. We cannot thank you enough for all you have done for us. We would never have been able to do this without your help. Thank you."

"I have your visas. Do you want me to keep them in the bank? They will be safe here."

"Yes, thank you. Do you know if Dora's girls are with her?"

"Yes, they came in this morning with all the children and staff. Dora is very happy."

Anna said, "About our money, do you know how we are going to Marseille?"

"Some of the routes are closed because of the war. There is no information yet. Do not worry. I will get the both of you to the ship if I have to take you there myself. Ladies, I have another person waiting for me. Keep in touch."

"Sonia, I think he adopted us."

"We could do worse."

"Let's go home and send a letter with the packages. We have a lot to tell."

"Let's stop for lunch at that café down the street."

"Sonia, I have not seen that tall boy for a while."

"Maybe he is in the army."

"I hope not."

"Next Monday, you start work, and tonight I have to go back to the theatre. Would you like to see the show? I can get you in at no cost."

"Funny!"

"Anna, we can just relax and wait till the war is over to get the train tickets."

Bucharest was getting crowded with soldiers from many different countries. After a while, it was easy to tell the countries from the uniforms. Anna and Sonia never saw a uniform from America.

Anna was getting situated in her job with the children but was not happy with the father. Sonia was having a grand time at the theatre. Sonia was saving money from the salary. Yankel was never called to join the army. Rabbi Morris Rosen became an army chaplain. He was stationed in Bucharest. Times had changed. But their little family had not. Dora would not let her daughters go back to Budapest. They were still living with her. The fighting had not come to Bucharest, and everyone was hoping it would not come.

Hanukkah and Christmas had come and gone. Everyone found it difficult to celebrate. They decided to celebrate New Year's at home and have their own party. The girls purchased hats, balloons, and whistles. A big cake was decorated like a clock with the hands pointing to 12. Furniture was moved out of the way, making room for a dance floor. Everyone got beautified. Rabbi looked handsome in his army uniform. Special wine was purchased for the New Year's toast. Everyone gathered in the sitting room waiting for the new bell to ring. To surprise Esther for Hanukkah, everyone chipped in and purchased Esther a new bell. She did not want to use it till New Year's. Today was the day. The bell was rung. Dinner was served. It was quite a feast.

Rabbi Morris said the blessing, and the special wine was toasted. This was Anna and Sonia's first taste of wine. Both girls did not care for it. Yankel and Antoine finished their wine. After dinner, the music was played. Everyone was dancing. Yankel took Esther for a dance. Everyone stopped and applauded. A good time was had by all. The year, on Monday, December 31, 1917, came in with fun and laughter at the Esther Trager house.

The Yiddish theater went on playing Yiddish shows. Sonia kept on working with the cast on the pronunciation of some Yiddish words. Antoine became a full professor at the University. On Tuesday, May 7, 1918, the Treaty of Bucharest ended the war for Romania.

Sonia woke up to whistles, horns, and firecrackers. She rushed over to Anna. "Something has happened. Let's go down and find out."

The girls went flying down the stairs. Someone grabbed her and gave her a long hard kiss. She was about to kick him when she saw it was Yankel. He handed her over to Antoine, He kissed her, and last, Rabbi Morris kissed her. The boys kissed all the ladies, even Esther. This was a big day, Tuesday, May 7, 1918.

Anna asked, "What is this all about?"

"The war is over for Bucharest. The world war will be over soon. The Germans are defeated."

Anna whispered to Sonia, "We can start making our plans to leave for America. Let's enjoy this day. The war is not over."

The weather was getting warmer. The snow had left, and today was a special day.

"Let's go and see if the Herastrau Park is open," Anna said. "Maybe the fairgrounds are open, and the carousel is running."

"Anna you are rushing it a bit. We can take a ride and see if the fairgrounds are open."

Sonia could have kicked Anna. She is not happy going to the fairgrounds. She did not like the amusements and especially the carousel. Everyone agreed to meet in one hour on the porch.

"Anna, remember to wear your walking shoes."

"Sonia, do you think we could go see Solomon? We can start looking into the train schedules. I am sure he is waiting for us."

"Come on, Anna, I do not want anyone waiting for us."

We all met in one hour and started walking to the streetcar. It seemed many other people thought the same. The fairgrounds were crowded. Many of the amusements were open, and the carousel was busy.

Anna said, "I am going on the carousel."

Sura and Faygie also went, and they seemed to be having a grand time. Sonia went over to one of the throw games. If you knock down all the bottles, you win a prize. She played one or two games but had no luck.

Yankel was standing behind her. He said, "Let me try. It will be a goodbye gift."

"Let me see if you can toss all the bottles off the table."

He knocked all the bottles on the first try.

The vendor said, "Lady, any animal on the rack."

Sonia picked the large brown dog. They went back to the group. There were a few other amusements. Sonia would not go on them either. The day went by quickly. They all climbed back on the streetcar that headed home.

Anna said, "Beautiful dog. Sonia, what are you going to name it?"

"I am not sure. What do you think we should name it?"

"Let's call him Brownie."

"That's a good name. He is Brownie."

People were celebrating till the next morning.

The next day, things quieted down and seemed back to normal. As the weeks passed, there was less and less war talk. Anna and Sonia decided to go see Solomon. They wanted to know if he had looked into train schedules. They were interested what route was the safest and the best way to travel to Marseille.

"Sonia, why don't we look into the traveling arrangements? We can get train schedules and map a way to travel. We know we go from Bucharest to Budapest, Hungary, from Budapest to Zurich, Switzerland, from Zurich to Marseille, France. We have to find out how many hours and/or days is each leg of the trip."

"Anna, our problem is we still have to wait till the war ends. Even then, we may not be able to get a ship. All the soldiers will be going home. The ships will be full."

"Let's go see Solomon."

"Anna, he will say we have time."

"He may be able to tell us how long it will take us to get to Marseille."

"Those are a lot of questions, Anna. Solomon will not be able to answer them until the war is over. Why don't we wait for a month or so and see when the war ends?"

"We are only guessing."

"Anna, I want to go to America as much as you do, but there is a war. I, for one, want to wait until it is over."

Their lives went on as usual. Sonia working at the theatre; Anna was working with the children. The new schedules were working beautifully. Sonia was about to leave to pick up Anna when she appeared at the door very upset.

"Anna, what is wrong?"

"I cannot work there anymore. The father keeps bothering me."

"What do you mean bothering?"

"You know, trying to touch me."

"Did anything happen?"

"I hit him in the face with a glass of water and walked out."

"Was his wife home?"

"Not yet. Let him explain why I left."

"Did the children see?"

"Yes!"

"Good for you."

That was the main discussion at dinner. Antoine and Yankel wanted to confront him. Anna said no.

"I am sure his wife will take care of him."

The summer was hot and quiet. There was no talk of the war ending. The British and the Americans were winning the war, but no sign of it ending. By mid-September, the girls were hearing rumors that the Germans were being pushed back to their own ground. Everyone was clinging on to every word in the newspapers. The war ended with the armistice on November 10, 1918.

The days turned into months. Everyone was aware this family was going to part soon. Yankel felt it the worst. He had feelings for Sonia and enjoyed having her near him, especially at the theatre. She was bright, funny, and very beautiful. The theatre was full every performance and finally making money. Sonia and Anna were having mixed emotions as well. They finally had a family again. Three and half years was a long time living in the same house.

Life was beginning to come back to normal. There were very few soldiers in the eating establishments and in the parks. The flowers started to bloom.

The girls were thinking about visiting Solomon. "Anna, let's visit Solomon at the bank."

"It is Thursday, and you do not have to work. I have not gotten a job yet. It works for the both of us."

"This is a good idea. I will bring the papers that he gave me. I hope he will explain how much money we have. I would like to leave some in this bank in case Papa runs out of money."

"That would be nice."

Sonya was wondering about traveling. "Girls, when are you thinking about traveling to America?"

Anna answered, "We thought we would send away for travel information."

Sonia said, "It all depends on the ships. They have to be released from the army. They were used as warships. Now they will be used to take the soldiers home."

"Let's see what Solomon has to say. We will go see him this afternoon."

"Sonya, come with us. This involves you as well. You must promise not to tell anyone where you were. Tell your mother where we are going today."

Sonya said, "I will be right back. I will tell my mother."

The three girls left the house and caught the next streetcar.

"Sonia, do you know where you are going," asked Sura.

"Yes, we have been there before. Just follow us."

The girls got off the streetcar and walked the few blocks to the bank.

They entered the bank, and Sonia asked for Mr. Solomon Bally.

The man in the red jacket said, "He is busy. Come back later."

Sonia was getting angry. She said, "You better take us to Mr. Solomon Bally, or I will have you fired." She then showed him the card.

"I am sorry. I was not aware that you are a special depositor. Follow me please."

The three girls were ushered into Solomon's office. He saw the girls coming and met them at the door of his office.

"Welcome, ladies. I was expecting you. This must be the other Sonya that is traveling with you?"

"Yes."

"Come in. We do have to talk."

"Solomon, I have to ask," said Sonia. "How is Dora?"

"Dora is fine. I saw her last evening. Her children left. Arrangements were made for them to go back home after the new year. Dora wanted a family holiday."

"Now, ladies, I do have news for you. I know you are anxious to be in America. I looked into ships and when they are sailing to America. You cannot get passage until April. All the ships are full of soldiers going home. There is one passenger ship going to Philadelphia. The ship is called the *Madonna*. It leaves out of Marseille, France. This is one of the first passenger ships leaving Europe. It departs April 20, 1918. It is scheduled to arrive in Philadelphia April 25, 1918. Sonia and Anna, would that suit you?"

"Yes. When can you book passage for us."

"Well, I am not sure. There are four forms of passage—first class, second class, third class, and immigration."

Anna said, "What difference does it make?"

"First class is very fancy and costs more money than you now have. We have to consider the trains. Second class is about the same as first class. Third class is less money but still expensive. So I booked the three of you in the immigration class. Sonia and Anna, your passage has been paid. You are of age and will have no problems."

Anna said, "Booked? You bought us tickets?"

"Yes. You leave Sunday, April 20, 1918."

Both girls jumped up and kissed him, one on each cheek.

Solomon said, "Now that is what I like. Now, Sonya Trager, I reserved passage for you as well. Did you get a visa?"

"Yes, I went the next day. Thank you for all your help and the two American dollars that was very helpful."

"You have to come back with your mother. I have a letter for your mother. It tells her what she must bring with her when she comes to see me. This letter informs her only of the cost of the ship. This does not include train fare."

"Speaking of train fare, Anna and I asked the train ticket master, 'How do we go from Bucharest to Marseille, France?' We told him that is where our family is going on holiday. We asked him for literature and/or train schedules. He nicely said he will look into train schedules. We asked what route is the safest and the best way to travel from Bucharest to Marseille, France. He was very helpful. He said this was the safest route. We should go from Bucharest to Budapest, Hungary, from Budapest to Zurich, Switzerland, from Zurich to Marseille, France. We have to find out how many hours and/or days is each leg of the trip. We can come back next Friday and pick up the schedules that he marked off for us."

Solomon was very pleased that the girls were working on their trip. "Are there any other questions, ladies?"

Sura asked, "What day is best for you and my mother to meet? My mother and I can come anytime."

"How about next Monday?"

"That will be fine. Thank you."

The girls left his office and proceeded from the bank.

Anna said, "How about some ice cream?"

They all agreed.

Sonia said, "How about looking at hats?"

Anna said, "That is even better."

Off they went; ice cream first and then hats.

Anna said, "What a wonderful day."

The girls just about made the ringing of the bell. Each one was full from the ice cream.

After dinner, Sonia said to Sura, "Please give the envelope to your mother."

"We will talk tonight."

"Good."

The group finished dinner. Faygie remarked, "What a beautiful evening. What shall we do?"

Yankel said, "Let's go for ice cream."

The three laughed. Sura decided not to go. She had a special letter to write. The others all went off to get ice cream.

Sonya and her mother met with Solomon. Sonya's ship and train fares were completely paid. At the closing of their meeting, Solomon thanked them for coming so quickly. This gave him more time to put together the train schedule. Sonya came home excited. Esther came home sad and wondering if she did the right thing.

Spring was approaching quickly. The theatre was full every night. The girls were getting quite good with their English and French. Sonia and Anna were putting away as much money as they can for traveling expense. The girls wanted to write home to tell them what ship and when they would arrive in America. Solomon suggested they wait until all the arrangements were finalized.

This was the first of March, and there was much still to do before packing. This day, the three girls went shopping for bathing suits. They knew the ship had a pool. This would be the first time the girls had a bathing suit.

Esther said, "There's a letter for you, Sonia."

The dinner bell rang, and everyone came to the dining room. The big discussion at dinner was the sea voyage and the size of the ship they were taking. Everyone knew the ship was called the *Madonna*, and it was a French ship. Esther announced that Sura was going to America with the girls. She was going to live at their aunt's house.

There was no performance tonight. Sonia and Anna excused themselves and went upstairs to read their letter. Anna opened the envelope. The letter was from Dora.

Dear Sonia and Anna,

I want to see you. Please come for lunch Saturday. Any time after 11:00 a.m. My children left yesterday for Budapest. They wanted to go to their own home. They were here quite a while. I was content knowing they were safe with me. I am still concerned about Budapest being safe. I do miss you. See you Saturday.

Dora

The girls decided to stay in their room for the night. They wrote a short note to Rada and home. They said,

Saturday, April 25, 1918, the ship the *Madonna* lands at Philadelphia, Pennsylvania, America. Please tell Aunt Pessy.

We will write more when we are at Aunt Pessy's.

Love, Anna and Sonia

"Anna, wake up. We have to be at Dora's at 11:00 a.m. What are you going to wear?"

"I have started to pack a pink sweater and a black skirt."

"I am going to wear a blue dress with long sleeves."

The girls rushed to dress. Esther was ringing the bell as the girls were walking into the dining room. The girls said they were invited to have lunch with Dora today. They had tea and a muffin and excused themselves.

They walked to the streetcar stop and waited for one to stop.

Sonia said, "Just think a few years ago, we had no idea there was such a thing as a streetcar. You know, Anna, we were greenhorns."

They got off and walked to Dora's house.

The butler said, "Good morning, ladies. You both look beautiful this morning."

"Thank you."

"The baroness is waiting for you in the garden."

As they entered the garden, Dora said, "I am so happy to see the both of you. I must say I missed you. We are having a guest. Solomon will be here soon. He has all your train tickets and the ship's boarding passes."

The butler announced Solomon.

"How are my beautiful girls this morning?"

"We are all fine."

"Let's go over all the tickets."

It took one hour for all the information to be explained to the girls.

Sonia said, "We understand. We have a few questions. The train to Budapest is about six hours. Do we have to take food with us?"

Dora quickly answered, "No, there is a dining car. You can go and have lunch or anything you want. Anna, there is a nice clean salon with a toilet that flushes. The dining car accepts Bucharest money. I made arrangements for my sister to meet you at the station and take you to her home. You will stay there for the two days until the train from Budapest to Zurich to Marseille, France, arrives. This is an overnight train with a stop in Zurich. Do not get off the train. Stay on the train. It leaves at 9:00 p.m. and arrives in Marseille at nine in the morning."

Solomon said, "A woman from the Banque de France will meet you at the large clock in the waiting room of the station. She will have information about your hotel in Marseille. She will have French money and American money for you. She will take you to the ship in the morning. She will make sure you get on the correct ship."

"The both of you have been so wonderful. We know we would not have been able to do this alone. I know Esther could not help us."

Dora said, "When I saw the two of you eating from a small basket, I became curious. When I saw that lady settle you in and leave the train, I was shocked. I was so glad you asked for direction to the toilet. I was happy to help. But I must say when I heard Anna kept flushing the toilet, then she asked about the water, I definitely wanted to know more about you."

"You both have been more than friends. You are family. We will miss you. We do have one last favor. Would you send a telegram to our aunt, giving her the time the ship arrives? Someone is supposed to meet us at the ship."

Solomon said, "I have sent instruction that a telegraph be sent to your aunt. I have her address."

"Thank you."

"Girls, I hate to rush you, but Dora and I have a dinner date and theater tickets this evening."

Both girls kissed them again and left.

After the girls left, Dora said, "Solomon, we have no engagements this evening."

"I know. If they did not leave, I was going to cry. No one wants to see an old man cry."

"You are unbelievable. Now that you mentioned dinner. You can take me out."

"Gladly, Baroness." The two of them spent a quiet evening together.

Meanwhile, the girls found a bench in the park and sat down. They could not hold back the tears. In a while, they composed themselves and got on the next streetcar home.

Dinner was served. Sonia and Yankel left for the theatre. The performance went smoothly. No one forgot a line. Yankel hurriedly closed up. They started home.

Yankel asked, "Could we stop for coffee and apple pie? This would be the last time we would be together."

Sonia agreed. She really wanted to go home. Sonia hated to say no to Yankel. They went into the coffee shop, sat down at their table, and ordered.

Yankel said, "Sonia, you really helped me. No one knows Yiddish like you do. I will miss that. Thank you for all your help."

"Yankel, you paid me for working. I know it was more than you would have paid anyone else."

"Yes, you are correct. Sonia, you do know I have feelings for you. Actually, it is more than feelings. I am in love with you." Sonia just sat there staring at Yankel. "I am asking that you not go to America. Stay here with me. Marry me."

"I am surprised and flattered. I am not sure how I feel about you. I am very fond of you, but I am not in love with you. I am sorry Yankel. I made a promise to my parents, to see them in America. I cannot go back on my promise. Would you mind if we left?"

"No, not at all."

They walked the rest of the way home without speaking. Sonia said good night. She went upstairs. This has really been a sad day.

The next evening, Yankel and Sonia went to the theatre for the evening performance. The girls were busy packing for the trip. They had to pack for the train and for the ship. Sonia packed during the day. Esther was helping Sura pack and crying while packing. The house was quiet. Everyone seemed sad.

Tuesday, March 15, 1919, Today

THE GIRLS WERE UP BEFORE the sun came up. They were still packing. They had a small case for the toothbrush and sundry items. They had to buy a larger case for their clothes.

Anna said, "What are you thinking about? You have been doing this for the last few days. Are you feeling well?"

"No, Anna, just sad. I never thought we would meet so many wonderful people."

Anna said, "Yes, I am going to miss them. Tell me about Yankel. Did he say anything about your leaving?"

"I will tell you all about it on the ship."

Anna said, "I was thinking about Dora. She is lonely. It is sad her children do not live closer. When Papa and Mama come to America, we are going to move close to them."

"I agree."

"Do you think there is something between Solomon and Dora?"

"No, just friends. He is Jewish. She is not. They are good friends."

"Do you think Esther is going to miss Sonya?"

"Yes. She is really going to be alone. We will have to help Sonya. She is going to miss being home. You and I had each other. We will always stay close."

"I wonder if Pessy's house is like this one?"

"We have been very lucky. Let's get dressed and go downstairs. Are you packed?"

"Yes."

"So am I."

The girls went into the dining room. The table was set for a Sunday breakfast. Esther rang the bell. Everyone came in slowly.

Antoine said, "We have an entire day. How do the ladies want to spend it?"

"How about our last day at the fairgrounds? Maybe Sonia can win a small dog to take with her."

"Anna, I am giving Brownie to Yankel. After all, he won it for me. Everyone meet here in one-half hour."

The day was completely enjoyable. Sonia went on a few amusements but not the carousel. Antoine won a large dog, and Yankel was lucky. He too won another prize. He chose a small mirror. He gave it to Sonia. At 3:30 p.m., they were on their way back.

They had an early dinner. The girls had to leave by seven. They were taking the streetcar. Everyone seated around the dinner table started to talk at one time. Rabbi wanted to know if there were postcards of the ship and to please send them pictures.

Yankel asked, "Is there entertainment on the ship?"

Sonia responded, "I promise to write and tell you all about the ship and send postcards."

Dessert was served. The ladies made a large cake for the girls.

Anna said, "It looks like a rowboat."

There was not a crumb of the boat left. There was no rush to get up from the dinner table. They sat and reminisced of the times that were spent together. The clock was ticking. It was 7:00 p.m. The girls excused themselves and went to get their suitcases. Yankel and Antoine helped the girls with their luggage down the stairs.

Yankel said, "I am going with you. These suitcases are too much for you both to carry."

At that moment, an automobile horn sounded once and then again. Sura looked out the door.

She said, "There is a man and a woman in the car."

Sonia went out on the porch. She shouted, "That is Solomon and Dora."

Solomon got out of the auto and went up the stairs to the porch. "Dora and I are here to take you to the train."

Sonia just hugged him. "Thank you, thank you."

Antoine and Yankel took the luggage and put it into the car. Dora came out to meet the girls' friends.

Solomon said, "We must go for they have to show their papers to the customs agents."

The goodbyes were difficult.

Yankel said to Sonia, "May I really kiss you goodbye?"

"Yes." And he did with all his heart.

Sura kissed her mother, both were crying. All the goodbyes were finished. The girls got into the car and off they went.

"What a pleasant and welcome surprise. Why didn't you tell us you were going to take us to the train?"

"We wanted to say goodbye again."

Solomon drove to the front of the train station. There was a porter collecting luggage.

Solomon said, "Girls, show him your tickets. He will put your luggage in your compartment."

Anna said, "Compartment!"

"Yes, this train has little rooms. The three of you are together in a compartment. Take a walk through the train. This is what the train to France is like and more. It is time to say goodbye."

"We will miss you," said Dora.

Solomon said, "You are the smartest and bravest young ladies I have ever had the pleasure to meet. Have a safe trip. Let us know when you reach Marseille."

The girls followed the porter to the train and to their compartment. Sonia handed the porter a paper bill. He thanked them and left.

"Well, Anna, can you believe we are on our way to America!"

PART 4

On Our Way to Marseille

SONYA SAID, "THE COMPARTMENT IS large. There are three sofas."

The conductor knocked on the compartment door. He entered and said, "May I see your papers please?"

All three girls opened the package and handed the conductor their papers and carefully replaced them into the packet. The conductor said, "Thank you, ladies," then left.

"This compartment must be for families. Sonia, what did you give the porter?"

"Solomon gave me a tip for the porter. Anna, that is for him bringing us our bags. He really thought of everything. I think he felt we were his children. He is not married and adopted us. When we get to America, we must send Albert and Alana a beautiful house present. We would have never gotten to America if it were not for him. He arranged with Solomon the entire money package. Solomon did most of the work. I think Solomon was aware he was having feelings for us. Sonya, how are you doing?"

"This is all strange to me. I have never been on a train before."

"Dora said there is a dining car. We should walk through the train. It will be like the one to Marseille."

"Sonya, did you bring something to read?"

"Yes, but I think I will just look out the window when the train starts."

"Later, we can go into the dining car and get a snack. We have till 9:00 a.m. Dora said her sister will be at the train to take us to her house."

Anna asked, "Will she have a red scarf?"

"No, Anna, I hope not."

Sonya asked, "What does a red scarf have to do with the train?"

"Nothing. It was just a joke."

The train gave a jerk and started off. The girls were on their way. Sonia started to read. Anna was doing a puzzle. The motion of the train made Sonya fall asleep. Sonia looked over to Anna, and she too fell asleep. Sonia continued reading her lesson book in English. Soon after, Sonia too fell asleep. The girls slept through the night. As the sun came through the window, the girls started to wake up.

Sonia said, There goes our walk through. We will be getting off soon."

Sonya asked, "I wonder if Budapest is anything like Bucharest."

"It might be a larger city. We will soon see."

The conductor came into the car and announced, "Budapest in twenty minutes."

The girls did not have much to pack away. They just sat.

"I will take out money for a porter if one comes into our car."

The train was pulling up to the platform and slowing down. A porter opened the car door and shouted, "Anyone need a porter?"

Sonia opened the compartment door and said, "Yes, we do please."

"Just you wait there. As soon as the train stops, I will be in to help you."

"Thank you," they said together.

The train stopped completely, and the porter was at their door. He gathered the suitcases, put them on a truck, and said, "Ladies, follow me." That is exactly what they did. He helped them down the steps and said, "There is a lady waiting for you. I will take you to her."

"Thank you," said Sonia.

They walked out of the station, and there was Dora's sister, waiting with the car door open for them. She waved to them and said, "I am Dora's sister. My name is Jeanne. Porter, please put the bags in the trunk. Girls, get in, and we can talk. I do not like talking on the sidewalk."

They all piled into the large auto.

Jeanne said, "This is Charles, my houseman. He will help you unpack some of the things you may need for just two days. Girls, tell me your names and something about you."

Anna went first. "I am Anna. The one sitting over on that seat is my older sister. Her name is Sonia."

Sonya said, "I know this is going to be confusing. My name is also Sonya, but I spell it differently."

"I will then call you Sonya with a *Y*."

"That would be fine," said Sonya.

Sonia asked, "Did Dora tell you anything about us?"

"Not really. She said she met three lovely ladies going to America and needing a place to stay while the train to Marseille arrives. That is just two days away. It is a lovely day today. So let's get you to my home, and the three of you get semi unpacked. We can then have lunch and maybe do a little sightseeing today. I know you are tired, so Charles, my houseman, will drive us around, and I will point out the sights. One month ago, you would not have recognized the city. It was full of soldiers and military equipment. It is almost back to normal."

"Was there any fighting in the streets?"

"No, all the fighting at that time was in Austria and Germany."

"Thank God."

"Oh, we are here."

They were driven to Jeanne's house. They quickly dropped their bags, washed to get the train's soot off themselves. They met Jeanne in the hallway. She was waiting for them. They got back into the car and were off to sightsee and lunch. Jeanne picked a lovely outdoor restaurant next to a river with the view of the main shopping area. The girls commented on the beautiful area. Jeanne explained the river is called the Danube. The waiter took their order, and in an hour, they were on their way to see the sights.

Jeanne started explaining that Budapest was really two independent towns called old Buda and Pest. They merged and became Budapest. It is now the industrial center of Hungary. Jeanne took the girls to the Buda Castle. She explained this castle was built in the thirteenth century and has two hundred rooms.

Sonya said, "You can get a load of borders in there."

The girls all laughed.

"It was built to protect the people from invaders."

Anna said, "Hajsyn can sure use a castle like that."

"Girls, Dora said you like to go shopping. Tomorrow we will go to Vici Street, have lunch, and go shopping. Walking will be good. You will be on the ship for five or six days."

Sonia asked, "Are there any milliners in that area?"

"Oh, yes. If you like hats, you will enjoy Vici Street."

Anna said, "That's wonderful."

"I know you did not get much sleep last night, so we will head back and get you situated in your rooms."

The houseman drove them back to Jeanne's house. She showed them to their individual rooms and to the salon that was in-between two bedrooms. Jeanne asked Anna and Sonia if they didn't mind sharing a bathroom.

They said, "No, not at all."

Sonya's bedroom and bath was across the hall.

"Dinner is at 7:00 p.m. I will see you then."

All three piled into Sonya's room. It was the biggest and had a sitting room attached. Sonya was amazed.

"I have never seen a room like this before." It has a bed with a top over it.

Anna said, "It is called a canopy bed. Dora has that kind of a bed in her room."

"Anna, how do you know that?"

"I passed by her room and looked in. The maid told me that type of bed is called a canopy bed. I am going to take a bath."

"All right, Anna. I will wait until you are finished. I will start a letter to Rada, Papa, and the family."

Sonya said, "I should write to my mother and the family as well."

"Say hello to everyone for Anna and me."

"I definitely will."

"We will meet here in the hall at 6:45 p.m."

Anna started to run the water when Sonia said, "This is a big house, but nothing like Dora's."

"Dora is a baroness. That house must have been in her husband's family a long time."

"I guess you are right. Let's get the letter started."

Dear Papa, Mama, Sol, Lou, and Reba,

Rada, I am writing one letter to all.

We are at Dora's sister's house in Budapest. We are waiting for the train to take us to Marseille. There is a two-day delay in our schedule. Papa, please tell Albert he is a true friend. Anna and I have been treated like family by Solomon Bally, the banker friend of Albert's. Solomon arranged all the legal papers, including sending a bank representative to help us get our visas. He even paid the two American dollars for the visa.

Remember I told you about a baroness. Her name is Dora. She too was wonderful. In fact, we are staying at her sister's house for the two days while waiting for the train to Marseille. Anna and I are fine. I am not sure we will be able to write till we are on the ship. We do not have a stop in Marseille. The ship will be waiting for us. Solomon has arranged for a woman from the bank in France to take us to the ship and make sure we are on the correct ship to America.

Just think, Papa, we are really going to America. Anna and I promise you, we will bring you to America as soon as we can. We all want the family to be together. I also promise, when you come to America, we will never be parted again.

Love to everyone, Sonia and Anna
Papa and/or Rada, have you heard from Boris?

Philadelphia

Pessy Samintsky Cohen

Pessy Cohen's home

"Mom, Mom, you got a letter from your sister in Ukraine."

"Oh, I've been waiting for this letter. Sam, give it to me please."

"What is this all about?"

"Remember I told the family. My sister Raisa, the one that lives in Ukraine, she has sent her two girls to America to live with us. They had to leave Ukraine. The girls want to bring their entire family here."

"The family is coming now?"

"No, only the three girls. The family will come next year or the year after."

"Are the girls staying here?"

"Yes."

"Mom, that is a lot of people. You, Pop, Lena, Philip, Anna and me—that is six people, and add three more. That is nine people. Wow, can you do that?"

"Yes, just add a little more water to the pot. She and Avraham paid our way to America. This is the least I can do. Raisa is my sister, and Sonia and Anna are my nieces."

"Mom, you said three girls. Who is the third?"

"She is the daughter of a friend from school. She never made it to America. She wanted her daughter to come here. She felt her daughter would have a better life in America. I need you and Philip to go to the ship and bring them here."

"When are they coming?"

"I don't know. I have to read this letter. Maybe it will tell us when. They are sailing on the twentieth of April out of Marseille, France, on the ship the *Madonna*. The ship line is Fabre Line. The ship is supposed to arrive on Friday, April 25 or 26 in the port of Philadelphia. We will have to inquire about the ship when it gets close to the date of arrival. Will you tell Philip, or shall I?"

"I will tell him. Philip and I have to take the day off."

"I will tell Pop that we are having guests, and you boys are going to pick them up. Pop knows the girls are coming. Well, we have about two weeks before they come. Where shall we put them?"

"Put them on the second floor with the bathroom between the two bedrooms."

"Thank you, Sam. That was kind of you. Now you can tell Philip he has to give up his bedroom. We have to buy an extra bed for one bedroom. The sisters can sleep in one room."

"I understand."

"Esther told me she will send money for Sonya's room and food."

"Mom, let's tell Philip tomorrow. I want to enjoy my dinner."

"I agree, Sam."

Budapest

Back in Budapest, it was approaching 7:00 p.m., and the three girls were walking downstairs. They made their way to the dining room. Jeanne was already seated. A server came out of the kitchen holding two trays of food. The houseman brought a few dishes of vegetables. The chicken was delicious, as was the entire meal.

The server said, "We have peach cake and vanilla ice cream."

The girls agreed to that dessert.

Jeanne said, "Let's go into the sitting room. I would love to hear more about you."

Sonia looked at Anna. They all followed Jeanne into the sitting room.

"Dora told me how she met you on the train to Bucharest."

Sonia answered, "We come from a small village in Ukraine. Our parents knew the war was coming, and they were concerned. Our mother has a sister in America. They thought it would safer in America. They also knew if we reached Bucharest, we would be safer there than in Ukraine."

Sonya told Jeanne her mother always wanted to go to America. She married a man from Bucharest and made her home there. "My father died three years ago. My mother decided that since her friend was sending their two girls to America, it would be company for me to join them. That is where we are now."

Sonia said, "We are excited. This is the last leg of our trip. Jeanne, have you ever been to America?"

"No, I never wanted to leave Budapest. This is my home. Dora and I were born here."

Anna asked, "Can you tell us more about Dora? We never wanted to ask."

"She was born and raised in Budapest in this house. Dora went to school and on to the university. She procured a position as a secretary in a barrister's office. She would often take her lunch hour in a café near the Danube River. When this extremely good-looking young man saw her sitting at a table alone, he asked if he could join her for his midday meal. He was not from Budapest and was lonesome. He explained he was a diplomat from Bucharest and was here on government business. Dora said, 'Yes, I would love company, but I must be back in the office in thirty minutes.' He asked Dora what type of work she did. She said, 'I am a secretary to a barrister a few blocks from here.' They finished their meal, and each went on their way. Dora was in the office when a young man entered. He announced himself. 'I am Baron John Farket. I am here to see Barrister Forester. Could you announce me?' The person at the front office said, 'I will call his secretary. Dora, there is a Baron John Farket here to see the barrister.' Dora opened the office door. And that was the beginning of a love story. They married and moved to Bucharest.

"Tomorrow, we will go to Vici Street, have lunch, and go shopping. Walking will be good. You will be on the ship for five or six days."

Sonia asked, "Are there any milliners in that area?"

"Oh, yes. If you like hats, you will enjoy Vici Street."

Anna said, "That's wonderful."

Sonia said, "I am tired. Let's all go to bed. Tomorrow will be an exciting day."

When they reached their rooms, they said good night to Sonya.

Anna asked, "Do you want to sleep with us?"

"Thank you."

Anna asked, "Did you write the letter to Papa?"

"Yes, I included Rada as well."

"Good idea."

"I will post it tomorrow. Let's go to sleep. I am very tired. Love you!"

"Love you too!"

Morning came, the girls were ready and anxious to go shopping. They met Jeanne in the dining room.

"Good morning, Jeanne."

"Good morning, girls. I see you are ready to invade Vici Street. Let's have a bite to eat, and we will be on our way. Our houseman is waiting for us at the car. Are we ready to go?"

"Yes!"

"Where would you like to go first?"

"The shoes shop, dress shop and, our last stop, the milliners. We love to try on hats."

Anna suggested, "Let's go up one street and down the other, and the shops we do not want, we just pass."

"Good idea."

Jeanne's houseman, George, let them off at the beginning of Vici Street. They all went into the handbag store. Sonya and the sisters each went in another direction. Each girl purchased a small cosmetic bag for lipstick, powder, and it could also substitute as a small evening bag for money and keys. Each girl got a different color. They all passed a number of shops that were of no interest. The next interesting store was a shoe shop. Anna was the most interested. She could use another pair of walking shoes. Sonya went into the cosmetic shop for lipstick. Anna decided to join her. Sonia walked and found a shop that had earrings in the window that she liked. But she did not buy.

Jeanne announced lunchtime. "This is my favorite café."

The girls entered. They were seated. The waitress handed them a menu. They all made their food and drinking selections.

Jeanne asked, "Have you ever eaten in an outside cafe?"

"Oh, yes," said Anna. "In Bucharest, there is a café near the amusement area that is shaped like a coffee cup. The handle of the cup is the entrance to the cafe. All the handles of silverware had a cup."

"That is interesting. When I go to Dora's, I will ask to eat at that cafe. If everyone is finished, we can continue on our way."

Sonia said, "Jeanne, we are paying for your lunch. That is the least we could do."

Jeanne thanked them. The dining slip was presented and paid. The girls were walking and looking in each shop. Nothing appealed to them. Sonia spotted a milliner's shop.

She announced, "I am going in there. Anyone else interested?"

Anna was right behind her. Sonya and Jeanne went along as well.

The salesperson said, "Can I help you?"

Sonia said, "Yes, I am looking for a cloche. Do you have any?"

"Yes, I do. Is there a color you would like?"

"Red would be nice."

The salesperson brought two hats from the storage room. Sonia tried it on, then Anna. Neither girl liked the color.

The saleslady suggested to Sonia, "I have a beautiful blue cloche that may be to your liking. May I bring it out?"

"Yes, please."

Sonia tried the hat on, and everyone said, "Sonia, that is your hat. It matches your eyes."

Sonia looked at herself in the mirror. She too loved it. "I will take this hat."

Anna said, "May I borrow it?"

"Yes, but do you mind if I wear it first?"

Everyone was tiring. Anna said, "My feet hurt."

Jeanne agreed it was time to go home. Jeanne waved a red handkerchief, and the houseman brought the car down the street. As they got into the car, Anna nudged Sonia. They both smiled.

Jeanne excused herself, and the girls went upstairs. Sonia went and read. Anna took a nap, and Sonya took a hot bath. Dinner was served at 7:00 p.m. The conversation was about the ship and how they were going to get to the dock.

Sonia said, "A woman from the Banque de France is coming to help us. She is escorting us to the ship. I guess Dora made those arrangements, maybe. No one told us."

"Jeanne, we want to thank you for housing and feeding us. Today was enjoyable. I got a beautiful hat as well."

Jeanne went through her mail. The three girls played card. The clock struck 10:00 pm.

Anna said, "I am going upstairs. I have a little packing to do. The card game ended.

Sonia asked Jeanne if she was going to be downstairs in the morning.

"I would definitely be there to see you off. I promised Dora I would take you to the train and actually seat you in your compartment. My houseman is driving us to the station."

We all said good night and proceeded up the stairs.

"Anna and Sonya, I think we should all be up, dressed, and fed before 9:00 a.m.

The Train Ride to Marseille and the Madonna

THE GIRLS ALL WERE UP and ready to leave by 9:00 a.m. George, the houseman, was waiting with the car. When Jeanne arrived, he started to put the luggage in the car. They all got in, and they were off. The station was not far away. In twenty minutes, they were at the rail station door.

Charles got a porter, and they proceeded to the train. They were able to board the train after they showed their documents to the immigration officer. The office was near their train. Jeanne and the three girls went into the office, showed their tickets and the documents. The agent stamped each document and said they could board the train. The train would depart in two hours. There was a brochure of the inside of the train. Each girl took one. They found a porter. He proceeded to show them their compartment. He placed the luggage in the racks above. Sonia gave him the tip, and he left.

Jeanne said, "Open the brochure. It directs you to number 3 dining car. If you look near the door to enter your car, you will see number 5. That is your sleeping car. When you are finished eating, you go back to car number 5. Read the remainder of the brochure, and it will give you all the information you need. If you cannot find something, pull this lever, and the conductor will come to help you."

Anna asked, "How about the toilet?"

"I think it is in this closet. Open the door." There definitely was a toilet.

Anna asked, "Does it flush?"

"Yes. Ladies, I have to leave you."

Sonia said, "Would you please write Dora and tell her we are fine?"

"Yes."

"Thank you, Jeanne. We appreciate all that you did for us."

"Sonia, I had a wonderful day with you ladies. Have a good trip."

Jeanne left the compartment and the train. She watched, waited until the train was out of sight, and left the station, thinking to herself, *I hope they have a good life.*

"Sonya, are you okay?"

"Yes, just a little frightened, Sonia."

"Please do not be. We have done this before. We are here. Please do not worry. Anna, let's play a game with that—" Someone was knocking on the compartment door. "Yes," Sonia answered.

"I am the conductor. Do you ladies need anything? Your mother told me to look into your needs. I am here to help you. Call for me anytime."

"Thank you."

Anna said, "Dora and her sister think of everything. Sonya, do you feel better now?"

"Yes."

"Now let's play cards. We can use matches for money."

The morning passed to afternoon. Anna was getting hungry. Sonia was tired, and Sonya was still concerned. The conductor passed through the car.

He bellowed, "The dining car is open for lunch." He knocked on their door and said, "There is a table set for you, ladies."

Anna said, "Thank you. Do you hear that? Shall we go? I am hungry."

They locked the compartment door. They followed the arrows to the dining car. The maître d' met the girls at the door.

He said, "Your table is the second on the right. That will be your table for the entire trip. Enjoy your meal."

Sonia said, "Dora must have told her sister to tip the conductor and the dining room. We never got service like this. Let's enjoy it. We may not get this on the ship."

The girls finished their meal and ordered dessert. Sonia ordered a cup of coffee. The day dragged on. The girls took a walk through the cars and stopped to buy a candy bar in the club car. They all started to read and, eventually, fell asleep. They would have missed their dinner if it were not for the conductor reminding them.

Sonia said, "During the night, the train will stop in Zurich, Switzerland, for an hour or two. Do not be upset. They will be dropping off or picking up passengers. Do not be upset, Sonya."

With that, the conductor knocked on the door. Sonia opened the door for him.

"I brought you blankets and pillows. Have a nice night, ladies."

Sonia asked, "May I tip you?"

"No need. Your mother tipped me and the maître d'. No tipping for you, ladies."

All three said, "Thank you!"

Anna said, "I told you Dora was involved."

Anna and Sonya fell asleep.

Sonia had more to think about. *What is it like on a ship? Is it big or small?* She had read that you could get seasick. Would she get sick like on the carousel? Who was going to pick them up? How would they know where to get off the boat? Many thoughts were running through her mind. She eventually fell asleep.

The Madonna

Max Gaidal

IT WAS A BEAUTIFUL SUNNY day. The girls were ready by 9:00 a.m. All the luggage was at the compartment door. The train was pulling into the station. The conductor came by.

He said, "Ladies, do not get off the train until a porter will come for you. I informed him to take you to the large clock in the middle of the station floor. Someone is waiting for you there. It was a pleasure taking care of you."

Anna said after he left, "He got a good tip."

They all seemed nervous. They had never been on a ship before or near an ocean. This was their biggest adventure.

The porter came and took their bags. He asked that they follow him to the large clock in the waiting room of the station. He left their bags on the cart and told the girls to wait there. Sonya and Anna got concerned.

Sonia said, "Solomon said a woman from the Banque de France will meet us at the large clock in the waiting room of the station. She will have information about our hotel in Marseille. She will have French money and American money for us. She will take us to the ship in the morning. She will make sure we get on the correct ship."

A young lady came running into the waiting room. She came up to Sonia. She said, "I assume you are Sonia?"

"Yes."

"I am Gabriel. I will take you to the hotel, and I will pick you up in the morning at 9:00 a.m. Please be ready. Solomon wanted you to get a good night's sleep and a bath before boarding the ship. Your ship accommodations are not the best. Porter, please follow us."

Gabriel found a taxi. She escorted the girls to the hotel. A bellhop took their bags to their room. She explained the procedure of getting on the ship. She handed Sonia and Anna an envelope with American dollars and French francs. Gabriel suggested they not go outside the hotel. There were shopping stores in the hotel. She explained the hotel bill was paid. Solomon said to tell the girls the money was for hats.

Gabriel asked, "What does that mean?"

"He means it is for shopping."

"I will pick you up at this room."

Sonia said, "It is okay, Gabriel. I speak French. I will still meet you here."

"Are there any questions?"

"No," said Anna.

"I will see you at 9:00 a.m. sharp here!"

"Gabriel, where are the tickets to the ship?"

"I have them. I will board with you, all right."

"Thank you."

The girls quickly took baths, dressed up, and went sightseeing on the street of their hotel. They returned for dinner in the hotel.

Anna and Sonia could read the menu. Sonya told them what she wanted, and Anna ordered for her. Sonia paid the dinner bill and left a tip. The waiter told them they could call for room service for a late dessert or for breakfast. After dinner, the girls stayed at the lobby of the hotel and did some shopping. The shops closed at 10:00 pm. That was when they decided to retire. Sonia and Anna slept in one bed, and Sonya slept in the other.

Sonya was up before the sisters. She dressed and was starting to repack when the girls woke up.

"I did not wake you for it was early. Sonia, call for room service, a pot of tea and basket of muffins."

The girls repacked, dressed, ate, and were ready before 9:00 a.m. There was a knock on the door. Sonia answered it.

"The porter is here for the baggage, but where is Gabriel?"

"I am right behind him. Are we ready to go?"

They followed the bellhop to the street where the doorman procured a taxi. They were off to the ship.

Gabriel said to the taxi driver, "The Fabre ship line port. We are going to the ship *Madonna*."

The girls were amazed to see such a large ship. They were not sure what to expect. They did not expect to see something that large. They all started to follow Gabriel to the dock.

Gabriel said, "Here are your papers. You must present them before you enter the ship. There is an officer at the top of the ramp. He will look at them and return them to you. Wait for me. I will go through after Sonya. I will take you to your stateroom. Your luggage will be put into your room later today."

No one moved at first.

Gabriel said, "If you do not walk up the ramp, you will miss the ship."

With that, Sonia started up the ramp. Anna followed her and Sonya after Anna. They all presented their boarding passes and stood on the deck of the ship waiting for Gabriel. She finally met them.

She said, "You are on the third deck. There are four decks on this ship. The bottom deck is the immigrant deck. They pay little fare and sleep and cook down there. You may get some of the cooking smells. That cannot be helped."

They walked down three flights of stairs and came to cabin 333.

"Girls, this is your stateroom."

Sonia opened the door. The girls entered their cabin. They were shocked to see a small room with three cot-size beds and a salon which had a toilet and extra-large sink.

Gabriel asked, "Are there any questions?"

Sonia said, "No. Thank you for all your help. We appreciate you help and getting us to the ship."

Gabriel said, "Have a safe trip."

Anna said, "This ship is not safe."

"No," said Sonya. "It is just like saying 'how are you'?"

Their suitcases have not arrived.

Anna said, "Let's go on deck and watch the ship leave France. Where do we eat?"

They passed a dining room at the stairway.

Sonia said, "Let's go upstairs. First, I want to say goodbye to Europe. Then we can explore the ship."

The ship's horn sounded, and the three of them jumped. The ship started to move. The three girls ran up the stairs and found a spot along the railing. People were waving to them from the dock. They waved back. Soon you could not see the people or the dock.

Sonia said, "Anna, we are off to America."

The three girls hugged together.

Anna said, "This is the beginning of a dear close friendship (which remained throughout their lives)."

The girls walked around each deck. They ended up on deck number 1. They noticed chairs were out with blankets. There were steps going up to a top deck. But there was a rope across the stairs. They walked down to the second deck. There again were chairs for people to sit and enjoy seeing the ocean. We went to deck number 3. There were no chairs. The girls stopped to watch the blue ocean. They decided to see if their luggage came. They came in time, for the luggage carrier was just delivering the bags.

Sonia asked, "When is dinner?"

"Down here, any time from 5:30 p.m. to 8:00 p.m. No reservations needed. It is buffet."

"Thank you."

He proceeded to put the bags in the cabin and left. The girls decided to keep the clothes in their bags except for any dresses that had to be hung. It was too early for dinner. They decided to go to the second level, find a seat, and watch the ocean. As they walked up the stairs, they heard music. They walked to the front of the ship. They saw people dancing and singing along with the music.

"This is lots of fun."

They found seats and watched the fun. Anna looked down and found Sonia tapping her feet to the music.

"Why don't you dance?"

"They are couples dancing. I would look silly dancing alone. Maybe they will play a hora. I will dance then."

They all watched and enjoyed the music.

Sonya said, "I am hungry. Let's see what is for dinner."

They left the second deck and went downstairs to their dining room. They found a table and then went to the buffet table. There was soup, sandwiches, salad, cut-up chicken, cut-up potatoes. There was a different table with cake, cookies for dessert. There were urns of hot tea and coffee. The girls proceeded to pick up a tray and follow the other passengers. Anna went up to one of the attendants. She asked for ice cream.

They said, "We will bring it to you."

The girls ate dinner and decided to stroll around the deck.

Anna finally said, "See, Sonia, you did not get sick. You get sick when things go around and around. This ship goes straight."

"Funny, Anna. You are right. I am not sick. Let's find a table and play some cards."

Sonya said, "I happen to have a deck in my purse."

"Great. There is an empty room next to the stairs. We can play there."

They found a table and chairs and started to play cards. They were enjoying the game when a group of young adults about their age asked, "What are you playing?"

"Poker," said Anna.

"We love the game," said one of the boys. "We are four. Can we join you? It's going to be a long five days to Philadelphia. This will help pass the time."

"We would love it," said Anna. "We do not play for money. We play for matchsticks. We could play for buttons."

"We will ask the steward," said one of the boys. "My name is George."

"My name is Karl."

"I am Hugo."

"They call me Liam."

Anna said, "I will start off. I am Anna. This is my sister Sonia. This is our friend. Her name is also Sonya."

George said, "The first Sonia, I am going to call you Blue Eyes. That will solve the problem. Are we all agreed?"

"Yes!"

The boys sat down, and the game began. Before they were aware of the time, it was past 10:00 p.m.

George said, "One more round, and that is it. Can we continue this tomorrow evening?"

"Yes."

The game ended as suggested. Everyone said goodnight and went their separate ways.

Sonya said, "Let's go on a ship next year if we can meet boys that way."

"Sonya, they too are going to a country where they do not know anyone."

"That's true."

"You have the key, Anna. Please open the door. I am very tired."

The room was quiet when Anna woke up. She had a dream about the tall boy that walked by the house in Bucharest. *I must have really been sleepy*. She got dressed and woke up Sonia.

"Get up. It is a beautiful day. Sonia, I had a strange dream last night. I saw the tall young man in my dreams."

"You must have been overtired to dream. Let's get Sonya up."

Sonya said, "I am up."

They were walking to the dining room when George saw the girls.

He said hello and then said, "How are you, Blue Eyes?"

Sonia answered, "Fine, thank you."

George asked, "Are we all going for breakfast?"

Sonia said, "We are. Are you?"

"Yes. My friends are on the next deck, getting the music ready."

"What music?"

"We have a recorder and records. We will be dancing and singing there later this morning."

Sonia asked, "Are we invited?"

"You definitely are."

They all ate breakfast, then proceeded to the second deck where the boys were setting up for the music feast.

George said, "They are ready. What would you like to hear?"

"Something you can sing along with."

Karl played a song, and people started coming and singing as well.

Anna said, "I am warm from dancing I am going to stand along the rail and watch the water."

Sonia said, "A group is starting to sing songs. I will be back."

Songs were being sung in French, Yiddish, Romanian. Boys and girls were dancing Czech polka, a Romanian hora, and the Russian Kizaki. By noontime the deck was popping.

The cool breeze felt good. Anna turned to get the full blast of cool air, and she saw this tall boy standing at the railing, looking out at the water. She thought to herself, *That is the boy in my dream. Could he be the one that walked by Esther's house?* Anna walked to Sonia where a group of friends were singing.

"Sonia, I have to speak with you."

Sonia became concerned when she heard Anna's voice. "Are you ill?" Sonia asked.

"No," Anna replied. "I am feeling fine. Do you see that tall boy near the railing? He was in my dream this morning. Does he look familiar to you?"

"No. He is very tall. I would remember him if I saw him some-where. If you think you know him, go introduce yourself."

"Sonia, I think he is the boy that walked by Esther's house."

"Go over to him and start a conversation. Ask his name."

Anna said, "He may laugh at me."

"Do you want me to go with you?"

Anna and Sonia walked to the railing where the young man was standing. Sonia tapped him on the back. He turned and said, "Good morning, girls."

Anna responded, "Good morning." Anna asked, "Do I know you?"

"Not really," responded the nice-looking tall young man.

Sonia took over the conversation. "This is Anna, my sister, and I am Sonia."

"My name is Max Gaidal. I remember your beautiful smile," he said to Anna. Anna blushed. "You dropped your scarf in school. I ran after you to give it to you."

Sonia said, "If you remember her, why didn't you go and speak to her when you saw her on the ship?"

"She was singing, dancing, and having fun. I didn't think it was right to approach her."

"Well, you are both here now. You can get acquainted. Anna, I am going to be with Sonya." She turned to Max. "There is another Sonya on this ship. We are with two boys, George and Karl, near the front of the ship. Come, join us."

Anna replied, "In a little while."

"Anna, I want you to join us real soon! Bring Max with you." Sonia turned to ask Max, "Do you sing?"

He replied, "I have no singing voice."

"Can you dance?"

"No, I am too tall."

Anna chimed in, "You are never too tall to dance. I will show you how so you can dance with me."

Max replied, "Thank you, Anna. I would like that."

"See you later in the front of the ship," said Sonia as she took off.

Max asked, "Would you like to sit in a chair against the wall, looking out at the water?"

"Yes, that would be nice."

Max secured two chairs and a blanket for Anna. He made sure she was comfortable. He then seated himself. Anna started the conversation.

She asked, "Why didn't you come and speak to me when you saw me on the ship?"

"I really didn't meet you. I just helped you retrieve your scarf."

Anna asked, "Are you going to America?"

"I am not quite sure. I may not be able to get off in Philadelphia because I do not have an American visa."

"How did you get on a boat going to Philadelphia and Providence?"

"This boat continues on to Cuba, then goes back to Marseille. I hired on as a waiter. I have a Cuban visa. My family is in Cuba now and sent me a visa." Max asked, "Can we spend some time together while we are on the ship?"

Anna replied, "I would like that. Max, tell me about yourself. Tell me about your family. Where did you live in Ukraine? Why are you going to Cuba instead of America?"

"Anna, I can only answer one question at a time." Max proceeded to tell Anna his story.

"I had to flee from the Ukraine army. They needed young boys to dig trenches for the soldiers. When the boys were finished digging all the trenches, they would kill them. They had no more use of them. My parents had to pay off certain people to get me out of the country. I got into Bucharest. That is the closest border to Ukraine. I spent three years in Bucharest, then traveled to Switzerland, then France. I was lucky to find a ship going to Cuba. The ship you are on goes to America and Cuba, then back to France."

"Before I leave the ship, I will give you my aunt's address in Philadelphia."

"Anna, we have three more days on board ship. Would you mind if we spend some of the time together?"

"Not at all. In fact, I would like to spend all the time with you. I want to get to know you."

"Anna," Max asked, "do you think you will ever come to Cuba?"

"Well, I'm not sure. Sonia and I have to get to America, then we have to find a way to get our parents, two brothers, and little sister out of Ukraine to America."

"Anna, tell me, how did you and your sister leave Ukraine? How did you get to Bucharest?"

"I'm sorry, Max. I promised my family I would never tell anybody. That includes you."

"I understand," said Max.

"Maybe when we are in America, we can talk about that adventure."

"I would like that. Would you like to go for a walk around the ship? It is a calm day. The ship is not rocking as much. I promise I will hold you so you will not fall."

"That would be nice. I must tell Sonia first. Come with me."

Max grabbed Anna's hand. She looked up at him in surprise. He said, "I promised you I won't let you fall, so I have to hold your hand."

They both started to laugh as they strolled across the deck. The ship started to rock. Max held her hand a little tighter.

He asked, "Are you all right?"

"Yes, as long as you are holding my hand."

Max spied Sonia. "Anna, your sister is at the front of the ship talking to George. I know him. We are both waiters on the dinner shift. I will see if I can have you as my guest for dinner one evening."

"How so, Max?"

"When the first-class guests leave the dining room, the waiters can eat. I will ask. Maybe I will be able to have you and Sonia eat with me."

"I know Sonia would love that. We will be able to get dressed up. That would be exciting. Sonia, Sonia," Anna yelled."

"I hear you. I was getting concerned. I was about to look for you. Hello, Max. Were you the young man who walked down our street?"

Anna answered for him, "Yes. Sonia, Max is a waiter on board ship. He waits on tables in the A La Carte restaurant for first-class passengers. He may be able to have us join him for dinner. Max said when the first-class passengers finish dining, the waiters are allowed to eat in that dining room. Max is going to ask Chef Andre if he could have a guest for dinner."

Sonia asked, "Is that allowed?"

Max went on to explain this restaurant was not managed by the owners of the ship. Jules Beau Approvisionnement (catering), a well-known French chef concession and his staff, is not part of the regular crew."

"Hi, Max! How was your day?" asked George. "Who is that pretty girl standing next to you?"

"George, I would like to introduce Anna Zitefsky."

"Oh, that is the one!"

Sonia chimed in, "That is my sister."

"I know, Sonia. I am teasing him."

Anna said, "That is not very nice."

"I am sorry, but I have never seen Max with any girl. I have been trying to get Max to introduce himself to Anna. I have never seen him so crazy about a girl that he has never met."

Max said, "I did meet her in Bucharest. I retrieved her scarf."

"Max, all this time, you were carrying a torch for someone you really only met once?"

"Yes," said Max.

Anna asked, "Is George a waiter in the same dining room that you serve?"

Max said, "Yes, he is."

"That would be nice if George wanted to ask Sonia to dine with us."

"I will ask Jules if that could be arranged. I have to go to work soon. I must get back and get dressed. We could not dine tonight, but I am sure Jules will allow us to dine tomorrow evening. I will see you tomorrow, Anna. Could you meet me where the deck lounges are on the first level?"

"Yes, I will."

"I am off from 1:00 p.m. till 5:00 p.m., after lunch till dinnertime. Then after dinner, I am free the entire evening. Is that a good time for you?"

"Max, I am free all evening. I will meet you whenever you are free."

"Thank you, Anna." Max and George walked off together.

The music stopped. The boys that were waiters left to dress for their job.

Anna said to Sonya, "Where have you been all day?"

"Look who is talking. You were the one that was not with the group."

"I know. It was wonderful."

"How was your day, Sonia?"

"I spent it mostly with George. We danced, sang, and ate bananas. I never expected to have such a good time on the ship."

Sonya spent the day with Karl. Sonya said, "It was a great day. Karl will bring the music equipment on deck again tomorrow. I told him I will meet him tomorrow. He said he will see me for breakfast. Do you mind?"

"No, no at all. As long as we know where we are at all times."

The stack horns blew, announcing dinner. The girls started to laugh.

Anna said, "I feel we are back at Esther's."

The girls went up to the first deck and sat on the lounge chairs the entire evening. They watched the sun go down. They listened to the slow dance music from inside the dining room.

Sonya said, "Someday I will go on a leisure ship and be in first class. I hope we can all say that."

Anna also added, "With Max."

Sonia said, "Anna, you really like him."

"Yes, I do!"

"Anna, come dance with me to this beautiful music."

The girls spent the remainder of the evening listening to the music.

Anna said, "They have ice cream machines on the second deck. Let's stop there before we go to bed." They all agreed.

The next morning, the girls were up and ready for breakfast. Karl joined them. He and Sonya left to set up the music. The odor from the kitchen in the level below was bothersome. Sonia remembered Solomon saying they were going to be on the immigration level on the ship. *I guess Solomon found out what that was, and he changed his mind. We must write to him at the bank and thank him.*

Anna said, "There was a horrible smell in the dining room."

"The last level of this ship is called the immigration level. They cook their own meals and do not have rooms to sleep. They only pay passage on the ship. Solomon told me we were going to be on the immigration level. I guess when he heard the type of accommodations, he changed his mind and paid to put us on this deck."

"Let's go up to the first level and wait for Max."

As the girls started toward the stairs, they noticed a chain across the steps. "I guess we are not allowed in that level."

They noticed they were setting up on their deck. The girls guessed that they were not allowed on the second deck either.

"Anna, don't worry. Max will find you when he hears the music."

Anna said, "I hope so."

The first dance was the hora, and they all danced. That got the party started. They were having a grand time. Came one o' clock, Anna started to become anxious. Max was nowhere in sight.

Sonia said, "Anna, you will see him. He is taller than anyone here."

Suddenly, he appeared, coming down the steps. Anna started to get up, but Sonia held her down.

"Let him come to you."

"Okay."

Max saw Anna and waved to her. He came and found a chair next to her.

Hello, Anna. How did you sleep?"

"Fine, and you, Max?"

"I thought of you all night."

Anna did not know how to respond to that. She said, "Thank you."

"Let's go for a walk, Anna. I want to know everything about you."

Sonia said, "Come back here in an hour. I want to know where you are."

"I promise to bring her back."

Anna and Max went for their walk. They found chairs on their deck and talked about everything. Anna did not say how she and Sonia came to Bucharest.

"Anna, I am sorry I cannot have dinner tonight. Jules said the last night on board ship, we can have dinner, the six of us."

"Max, that is wonderful. I will tell Sonia."

"George said he will tell her."

Max and Anna spent the next three days together walking and talking. Sonia and Sonya spent the following days dancing, singing, and eating bananas.

Sonia said, "I never want to get off this ship. I will remember this for the rest of my life."

On the fourth day, Anna insisted Max and she join the dancing.

"Max, I understand you cannot carry a tune and do not want to sing. You can learn how to dance. Come, I will teach you."

After Max stepped on Anna's feet a few times, he was getting the idea and was actually enjoying dancing.

"Remember," Max said, "Tonight at 8:30 p.m., dinner. I will come for you. Otherwise, they will not let you on the deck."

The three girls left the deck at 5:00 p.m. and started to bathe and dress for dinner. At exactly 8:15 p.m., Max was knocking. Anna opened the door.

Max just stood there. He said, "You are beautiful."

Anna said, "Thank you."

And off went the three girls and Max. Max did most of the serving, and the evening was enjoyed by all.

The two Sonias and the boys decided to play cards. Anna and Max decided to walk around the deck and find a seat.

Anna said, "Max, here is my address in Philadelphia. Please write to me. I want to know where you are."

"I promise I will write to you when I have an address." Max said, "Don't forget me."

"How can I? I dream of you."

"I will see you before you get off the ship."

He walked Anna to her cabin. He bent and kissed her on the cheek and left.

The girls were dressed and packed. The ship was to dock at 10:00 a.m. Passengers were to go through customs at noon. The three boys said they would help them with the luggage.

"Let's go and see the ship dock. That should be exciting. Our first glance of America."

The ship was stopped in front of the docks. It was not entering. The captain was on the loudspeaker.

"This is the *Madonna*. We are to dock in Philadelphia at 10:00 a.m. What dock do we pull into?"

"Sorry, Captain, we are full up. We cannot accommodate your passengers. Take them back to France."

"Like hell I will! They paid their fare and are going to America. Call the dockmaster in Providence. Tell them we are coming in tonight."

People were gathering on the deck. There was a lot of commotion. Passengers were saying the ship cannot stop in Philadelphia. The girls were getting upset.

"What can we do? Where would we go?"

Max said, "I will find out what is happening. You can always go to Cuba with me."

An announcement came over the loudspeaker. "Ladies and gentlemen, this is the captain. We cannot dock in Philadelphia. The docks are full, and customs cannot handle all the passengers. I am going to our second immigrant departing station. We will be in Providence this evening. We have informed the families of the passengers where the ship will be docked and where the passengers will be disembarking. Please understand your families will be there for you."

The ship docked in Providence that night.

The girls were to spend another night on the ship. They were upset and sad. Max stayed with Anna till 5:00 p.m. He had to go to work. The girls were concerned. Their luggage was in the lockers, waiting to be taken off the ship. They had nothing but what they wore. They were able to sleep in their cabin. The morning did not come fast enough for them.

The girls decided not to eat. They went to customs and got approved to depart when their area was called. They waited near the ramp. The girls were next to disembark.

Sonya said, "See you on the platform where our luggage is stacked." Anna and Sonia were behind her as they walked down the ramp.

Meanwhile, Philip and Sam took their time getting to the docks. They lived only a few miles from there.

Sam said, "Where are we going to put three girls? We got moved out of our rooms."

"I hope they are good-looking."

"Philip, that is all you think about."

"What else is there?"

They parked the car and started to the dock when they heard a loudspeaker. They could not make out what the person was shouting. As the boys got closer, they saw people standing on the platform in front of the docks, talking with one another.

Sam stopped and asked, "Would you know where the *Madonna* is docked?"

The gentleman next to him answered, "Providence, Rhode Island."

"What? Are you sure?"

"Yes. All these people were waiting for the ship. The dockmaster would not let the ship in. They have to go to Providence, their home port. They will be there late tonight. They will go through customs in the morning."

Philip said, "Let's go home and grab some clothes, gas money, and go to Providence."

Sam and Philip told Pessy the problem. She gave them gas money, and off they went. The trip was over 230 miles. They reached Providence that evening and checked into a rooming house for the night.

They found out the ship was docked, and passengers would disembark at 10:00 a.m.

Sam said, "Let's get there early so we can see the girls when they walk down the ramp."

Philip agreed. They parked the car and walked to the docks. Passengers were starting to disembark—first class, second class, then third class. They knew the girls were in the third class. They were watching the people walk down the ramp. At the top of the ramp, Philip saw three girls walking down the ramp. Sam looked up. He saw this girl walking down the ramp.

He said to Philip, "See the one on the right?"

"Yes."

"Philip, do not bother her. She is mine! I am going to marry her!"

Photo believed to show the victims, mostly Jewish children,
of a 1905 progrom in Yekaterinoslav (today' Dnipro)

Avraham (Abraham) Zitefsky

Raisa(Rose) Saminsky Zitefsky

Pessy Saminsky Cohen

Anna
Zitefsky

Sonia
Zitefsky

Max Gaidal

Louis (Lou) Zitefsky

Solomon (Sol) Zitefsky

About the Author

NORMA COHEN GITTELMAN IS MARRIED to the same guy for sixty-six years. They have raised three remarkable children, and they have given them the pleasure of enjoying eight grandchildren. She is an accountant by trade. She has dabbled extensively in politics. Her hobbies are painting, sculpture, and stained glass. She and her husband have traveled throughout the world, but there is nothing that can compare with the good old United States of America.

She had wanted to write this book about her mother and her sister's coming to America and their desire to bring the remainder of their family to America. They have left them with the knowledge that family is important.

Lightning Source UK Ltd.
Milton Keynes UK
UKHW012312250921
390927UK00017B/464/J